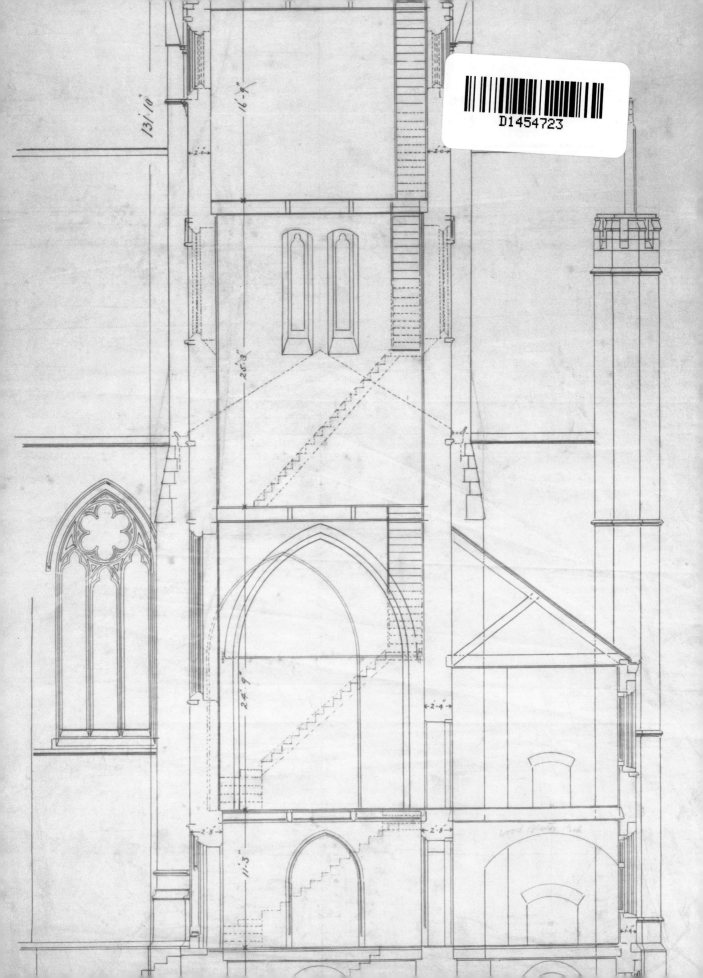

# THROUGH THE GATES
## INTO THE CITY

# THROUGH THE GATES INTO THE CITY

## A Metropolis, a Seminary and a Chapel

TIMOTHY A. BOGGS

PHOTOGRAPHY BY BRUCE PARKER

PREFACE BY SAM WATERSTON

Published by The General Theological Seminary of the Episcopal Church
175 Ninth Avenue
New York, New York 10011

AUTHOR: Timothy A. Boggs
PHOTOGRAPHER: Bruce Parker
DESIGNER: BTDNYC / Beth Tondreau assisted by Suzanne Dell'Orto and Kyung Li Kim
PHOTOGRAPHIC ASSISTANCE: Chad Rancourt
COPY EDITORS: John Douglas and V. K. McCarty
PROJECT MANAGEMENT: BTDNYC
PRINTER: The Stinehour Press, Lunenburg, Vermont

Typeset in Bembo and Gotham Book

*This book is dedicated to the ministry of the Guilds of Chimers, Precentors and Sacristans. For generations, these gifted students have joyfully brought to life the worship of God and the building of the community of The Chapel of the Good Shepherd.*

# PREFACE

## Sam Waterston

EVERY BUILDING IS BOTH SHELTER AND SPEECH. The Chapel of the Good Shepherd at the General Theological Seminary is a pre-eminent example. It functions every day as the gathering place at the center of the seminary's life, and it says a great deal about its builders' understanding of worship, of a house of God—even about the builders' idea of the nature of God. The Chapel does all these things beautifully, in expected, and unexpected, ways.

The text and photographs in this fine book will tell you a great deal about this building's warmth, its dignity, its volume, its grace and its strength. You will also learn quite a bit about the Chapel's history, and the generous gifts of time, talent, and treasure that built it.

Before I got to know the General Seminary, I wandered into the Close one Sunday morning looking for a church service. As it turned out, I had arrived at the one time when there would be none (for the wonderful reason that all the seminarians were assisting in their parish field placements throughout the City). If you sit there alone for a while, as I did that morning, you may find the Chapel has much to say to your soul, even without benefit of a service.

Later, after I had become a part of the Seminary's extended community of friends, I joined with hundreds of others in attending a Eucharist at which Archbishop Desmond Tutu was the preacher. Then, the glories of the organ, the choir—and the preaching—nearly took the roof off this venerable structure. It was a worship experience I shall never forget.

Full or empty, the Chapel's orientation doesn't change: at the center of things, looking south, its doors famously open to the city, with a message carved into the steps—lest we miss the point—declaring it a gateway for coming into the life of the spirit and going out into the life of the world. Since I read this book and learned about that carving, it's impossible for me to look at the Chapel without thinking what a wise and far-sighted message it is, for a Seminary in a City.

I hope you are as pleased with this book as I am to introduce you to it. May it inspire you to come and hear for yourself what the Chapel has to say.

# ACKNOWLEDGMENTS

I AM COMPLETELY RESPONSIBLE for all errors of fact or judgment in this book. However, many people get credit and thanks for their help in giving it whatever value it may have.

First, thanks to Bruce Parker, a wonderful collaborator, a good friend, a great photographer and an extraordinary gift to General Seminary and the Church.

Thanks to Sam Waterston for gracing this book with his words and for his dedication to General Seminary.

Special thanks to R. Bruce Mullin, my faculty advisor on this project for his encouragement and guidance and to J. Robert Wright, my academic advisor, who provided painstaking and dedicated help in reading and advising on this work. Thanks to a great teacher, Ronald Young, in whose course this project was nurtured, and to Richard Corney, David Hurd, John T. Koenig, Emily Knox, Margaret Schwartz and Samuel White for their perspectives and help.

Thanks also to Thomas Boggs, Charles Connelly, Tom Crisp, Patricia Curtis, Roger Gentile, Donald Gerardi, Elizabeth Leber, Kathleen Mikkelsen, Bruce Ragsdale, Anne Rieselbach, Stephen Shaver, J. Gregory Tallant, Emily Tallant, Andrew Walter and Susan Walter for reading an early draft and offering so many constructive suggestions.

Designer Beth Tondreau was a joy to work with and provided essential creativity.

Great thanks to Chad Rancourt for hours of professional assistance.

Warm thanks to John Douglas and V.K. McCarty, the most amazing copy editors.

And extra thanks to the incredible editor James Schwartz. It's so good to have such a talented wordsmith in the family. His contribution was incalculable.

Thank you all.

## A Chapel in a City

THE CHAPEL OF THE GOOD SHEPHERD stands proudly at the heart of The General Theological Seminary, its red brick and brownstone bell tower rising more than 130 feet into the Manhattan sky. Viewed from the Seminary's second entrance on Twentieth Street, the Chapel's portal has a double function and a double meaning. It is both a central part of the internal design and spiritual life of the Seminary, and an open door—a conduit between the intimate sacred space within and the larger Church and city beyond. Rather than facing inward as a traditional collegiate chapel might, or standing opposite the main entrance to the Seminary, the Chapel looks outward, into the southern light, beyond the lawns to the city itself.[1] As the contemporary New York architect and expert on the Seminary Samuel White put it, "This very fine entrance turns her shoulders to the east and west portions of the Close, revealing herself only to one who turns to face her directly, or to one who approaches from the outside entirely."[2]

This unusual but deliberate twist, planned and executed more than a century ago, enables an ecclesiastical building of the highest architectural quality and enduring character to serve as a bridge linking the quiet lawns and classrooms of a theological community with the thriving secular life of the metropolis outside. Building such a bridge, forging such a relationship, is an essentially religious exercise. Two different cities thrive here: the complex city of daily human life, community and commerce, and the eternal city of God.

The Chapel stands on a small corner of the city of God, but squarely in the midst of urban life. Several observers have noted that the Chapel's entrance explicitly "recalls a medieval city gate."[3] Such gates, with their arches pointed upward in the grand Gothic tradition, created symbolic thresholds, liminal spaces that invited people to pass between these different worlds. Revived and adapted, but still in use in this Chapel many hundreds of years later, these Gothic lines shape an enduring and deeply theological intention. The Chapel is always open and unlocked, the inviting portal welcomes all.

## Hoffman's Dream

FROM ITS INCEPTION, the character of the Chapel of the Good Shepherd—a sanctuary called by the New York City Landmarks Preservation Commission "the jewel of Chelsea Square"—reflected the ambitious dreams of Eugene Augustus Hoffman, the visionary and generous Dean of the Seminary from 1879 until his death in 1902.[4] For him, the Chapel was the keystone in a larger plan to establish The General Theological Seminary as a finely designed, stable and enduring institution for training leaders of the whole Church. Its construction would remove once and for all any doubt about the Seminary's viability and presence in the heart of urban America. Moreover, it was part of a broader effort to shape the nature of the Episcopal Church by maintaining a thriving and rigorous general seminary, one that could remain largely free from the vagaries of regional, ecclesiological and theological extremes. Realizing these lofty goals entailed a deep struggle within the Church, a struggle that touched on the continuing question of the Church's place in the world and the place of theological education and ministry in the heart of urban and national life.

Periods of calm at The General Theological Seminary have frequently been interrupted by painful controversies and struggles. These challenges reflected the

By the end of the century Chelsea Square had a confident and complete quality. The East Building, on the left, was replaced in 1892.

complexities of theological and ecclesiastical life in a national and global church, as well as the conflicts that inevitably arose between large personalities living in a small community. The stress and tumult of a burgeoning metropolis presented fundamental problems in the middle of the nineteenth century. Unsettling fluctuations in the national and local economies directly impacted the school's financial health. Persistent critics challenged the Seminary's very existence and future in Manhattan. By the turn of the twentieth century, many of these challenges had been aggressively addressed, both theoretically and tangibly, by the funding, design and construction of an ensemble of remarkable buildings. In these buildings, with the Chapel at their center, seminarians and the Seminary itself would live, grow and shape an enduring relationship with the city and the Church.

The construction of the Chapel and the creation of the campus were intentionally bold statements. Laying the cornerstone of the Chapel underscored the fact that the Seminary and the Church would firmly remain in New York and continue to grow and change, just like the city outside the gates. Further, the building of fine and enduring spaces for worship demonstrated the commitment of the Church at large to a *general* clerical education set firmly in the broad middle of the various theological, regional and partisan positions that have and will continue to challenge the denomination. This is an Anglican way, a tradition of the community holding divergent views in tension while finding common ground in the actual practice of the faith. The Chapel and the ensemble of buildings stand as visible symbols of a commitment to Anglican tradition and theology, and to the English style and the commitment to reason that accompanies it.


## *Chelsea Square is Born*


FOUNDED IN 1817 BY THE GENERAL CONVENTION, the governing body of the Episcopal Church, The General Theological Seminary was the first seminary established by the Episcopal Church of the United States. On May 27 of that year it was resolved that:

> it is expedient to establish, for the better education of the holy orders
> in this Church, a general Theological Seminary, which may have the
> united support of the whole Church in these United States, and be
> under the superintendence of the General Convention.[5]

As one of the world's first Protestant seminaries, General was a part of a movement that took the education of clergy out of traditional colleges and placed it in specialized and separate schools. In the spring of 1819, the Seminary held its first classes in rooms of St. Paul's Chapel on lower Broadway. In 1820, the Seminary moved to New Haven where it remained until 1822, when it returned to New York City and leased rooms at St. John's Chapel in Varick Street.[6] In 1824, the Seminary decided to build its own buildings on land north of the commercial heart of the city, a completely undeveloped block that would come to be known as Chelsea Square.

The Seminary block had been donated to the Episcopal Church by the primary Chelsea landowner, Clement Clarke Moore, in 1817. Moore, best known as the author of "A Visit from St. Nicholas," was the son of Benjamin Moore, a President of Columbia College and New York's second Episcopal Bishop.[7] His estate comprised the area between the south side of Twenty-Fourth Street and the north side of Nineteenth Street, from Eighth Avenue to the Hudson River. (In the mid-nineteenth century, the riverbank was roughly one hundred feet east of the present Tenth Avenue.) The property contained approximately sixty city lots.[8] One historian noted that "Once resistance to lower Manhattan's northern spread

proved futile, Moore had decided to make the best of things and systematically developed Chelsea as a fashionable quarter, anchored by the green grounds of the General Theological Seminary."[9] Moore's commitment to the Seminary included serving on the faculty as a professor of biblical languages from 1821 to 1850.

The Seminary's first building, known as the East Building,[10] built in 1827, was designed in the Gothic Revival style. At its heart, this movement reflected a respect for and romantic connection to the past. Noted architectural historians Marvin Trachtenberg and Isabelle Hyman write, "There remained in England a bedrock of deep-seated religious, national and emotional attachment to its Medieval buildings. All through the period of the English Renaissance and Baroque architecture, the Gothic style continued to be used especially for ecclesiastical and collegiate structures."[11] Building on this tradition, a genuine nineteenth century revival occurred, drawing on a fresh scholarly and literary understanding of Medieval style while taking advantage of profound technological advances in building techniques. In both Britain and America this revival was enormously significant; it rekindled interest in much of the architecture of Europe by endowing it with new intellectual and spiritual life. Gothic Revival buildings drew on "a new architectural accuracy, imaginative depth and ambition."[12] The

Gothic Revival in architecture, particularly in religious and academic settings, as Émile Mâle showed in his now-classic 1913 volume, *The Gothic Image,* was replete with biblical, natural, and archetypal symbols.[13] "Inside and out, Gothic Revival provided a virtual history, with nature and the spiritual life entwined in harmony and symmetry, reflecting sensations of security and purpose."[14] Once the ideas of Gothic Revival took hold in England and America, the key elements of its aesthetic were widely explored and realized. The leading New York architecture critic Montgomery Schuyler would note, "The Episcopal Church was the most judicious American patron of this architecture."[15]

At Chelsea Square the new Gothic Revival buildings were built of Manhattan schist, the extremely strong 450 million-year-old bedrock of the island quarried in several locations, including nearby Pitt Street. The second Seminary structure, the West Building, was closely modeled after the first (which no longer stands today) and opened in 1836. The New York City Landmarks Preservation Commission asserts that the building represents an early and "a fine example of Gothic Revival architecture" and is not only the oldest building in the present Chelsea

Historic District, but one of the oldest continually occupied public buildings in the city.[16] When it was erected, the Hudson ran less than a few dozen feet from its doorway.[17] Faced in rough-cut stone, the West Building displays closely modeled joists and buttresses marking the corners, and a fine long façade divided into three sections.

Now some 170 years old, the structure was remarkably well built. The fact that it has weathered the years so well says more about the great care that was taken in its design and construction than it does about the attention to repair it has received in subsequent years. One can imagine the early uninterrupted views from the upper floors of the fine East and West Buildings, whose western and southern windows must have provided wonderful light and captured classic early nineteenth century Hudson River vistas. Across the river on the New Jersey shore magnificent grassy wetlands with egrets and herons were part of a dynamic ecology that included the richest oyster beds in the world.[18] A number of etchings and paintings suggest an almost bucolic setting in middle and northern Manhattan during this era. This would not last long, as entrepreneurs noted that "plenty of land awaited development on the rolling countryside north of Fourteenth Street."[19] Manhattan

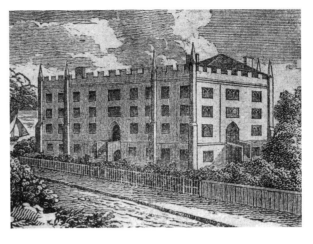

In the early 1800's, prior to major landfill, the Hudson flowed near the West Building.

land values had risen 750 percent between the Revolution and the War of 1812 and continued to climb as the city became central to American culture and commerce.[20]

At their opening and for the next decades, these two grey stone buildings housed nearly all the residential, educational, administrative, library and worship needs of the Seminary. For fifty years before the consecration of the Chapel of the Good Shepherd, a stuffy crowded room in the West building would serve as a place of worship for the seminarians and faculty. Although some faculty lived elsewhere in suites of rooms or private houses, students and most staff essentially spent their entire Seminary experience in these two cramped buildings, which became completely inadequate, with insufficient space, poor ventilation, and erratic interior lighting and heat. No doubt, all contributed to a "hot-house" environment that must have exacerbated normal community stress and affected the health and character of the Seminary.

## The Forbes Battles

IN MAY 1869 THE TRUSTEES, AS WAS THE CUSTOM, chose a faculty member for the position of Dean. Although elected as the first "executive Dean,"[21] the term of the Reverend John Murray Forbes nearly closed the Seminary in the city. Seminary historian Powel Mills Dawley refers to him as "a sad mistake . . ." and notes, "One less able to deal with the rising challenges . . . would have been hard to find."[22] Forbes, the second choice of the Board of Trustees, enjoyed the support of neither the powerful Bishop Horatio Potter of New York, nor the rector of the prosperous and powerful Trinity Church, the ardent and energetic Dr. Morgan Dix. Dean Forbes was an erratic leader. Often absent for long periods, he was a severe disciplinarian when present on campus. Nowhere was his strident tone more evident than in his adamant opposition to Catholic ritual.

Forbes believed the Seminary had to be removed from the secular, moral and Roman Catholic influences of the city and the dangers of the Ritualistic movement within the Episcopal Church. This Ritualism could be seen in some ways as a second phase of the earlier "Oxford movement," in that it emphasized the Anglican connection to the Catholicism of the Medieval and Patristic periods. However, the ritualists derived their inspiration as well from a Cambridge University movement that followed Oxford Tractarianism. The Oxford Movement had so severely roiled the Church and the Seminary for decades that Forbes was on high alert for any remnants of unorthodox practice, which he believed were fueled by influences in the city. The Oxford Movement and the later Ritualism called for more elaborate ceremony and raised the stature of the clergy while increasing the use of music and hymns.[23] In his Report to the Board in 1871 he summed up the views that he had been adamantly voicing for years within the Board and Church circles:

> I am very concerned. In the proper and strict senses of the terms the Seminary is not and never has been and never can be made a proper training school for Ministry until isolated from the excitement and turmoil of the great City, withdrawn from the distractions of almost every kind of doctrine and every kind of practice to be found in the Church and out of the Church.[24]

Dawley asserts, "The bitterest times of troubles in the Seminary's history came in mid-century."[25] This bitterness remained throughout Forbes' four-year term and focused in large measure on the continuance of the Seminary in Manhattan.

The Forbes faction on the Board expressed financial, educational, moral and ecclesiastical objections to maintaining the Seminary in the city. And they nearly succeeded in removing it. A special committee of the Board had been created early in Forbes' tenure to consider how to proceed. Calling themselves The Committee on the Removing of the Seminary, they had apparently reached their conclusions before considering the case. "For many years, a strong desire has been felt to remove the Seminary from the City of New York," they noted within weeks after organizing.[26] They retained legal counsel to advise them about options permitted under the conditions of Moore's donation, and discovered that removal from the city was permitted.[27] Then they sought advice from bishops and churchmen well outside the orbit of Seminary life. New special committees were established including one called "The Special Committee on the Seminary Block" which concluded that the property could be entirely leased or even sold for use by secular parties. In 1871 they advertised in various city publications "for the sale or lease of the entire Chelsea Square block and river frontage."[28] Fortunately, a recession in the city economy resulted in very few responses to the offer.

Another special committee established by Forbes considered merging the Seminary with the Episcopal Columbia College and The Protestant Episcopal Public School, a secondary school of the time, "with a hope of creating a proper

Church University," like Oxford or Cambridge outside the city limits.[29] Dean Forbes even went to some lengths to become a thorn in the side of the city government; claiming, for example, that their decision to establish the new Ninth Avenue elevated train with a station in front of the Seminary was an affront. "This new intrusion, just feet from our gates affirms we are out of place in the business part of the city . . . surrounded by dwellings, stores, taverns, and manufacturing, passed by steamboats and traversed by railroads on either side, at all hours of the day and night amidst the general hum of business and the excitements of pleasure and the inducements of idleness," he wrote.[30] Forbes looked close to home for any excuse to move the Seminary, reporting to the Board in detail on the purported ill health of many students, which he attributed to the poor quality of air and water in the city.[31] (His successor would report within one year of entering office on the fine health of the student body, noting the "salubrious quality of life in Chelsea.") Some faculty members supported Forbes' plans. A report to the Board on Student Discipline and Instruction mentions that, "Your Committee believes removal of the Seminary to some quiet neighborhood, free from the city's distractions and . . . evil pursuits" would improve the students' discipline and educational environment.[32]

Led by Forbes, the Standing Committee accepted the gift of a new site for the Seminary: fifty-five acres of land in Mamaroneck with views of the distant Long Island Sound and the "fine atmosphere of the hills and vales of Westchester," just a few dozen miles outside the city.[33] But the Seminary stayed put because

Jewish students and neighbors join a Chapel service in memory of the Holocaust.

Then Presiding Bishop Edmund Browning, third from left, and other Bishops celebrated Eucharist on the Centennial of the Chapel in 1988.

Forbes (and his committee) faced powerful opponents. These included Dr. Dix of Trinity, and Forbes' nemesis on the faculty, Professor George Franklin Seymour, a longstanding church history don, well connected to the faculty, the students and the wider Church. Seymour would later become Dean and the first Bishop of Springfield.

The failed attempts of Dean Forbes and his camp to move the Seminary seem to have been prompted by a mix of anxieties, some that he shared with others in the Episcopal Church. Having lived through the intense turmoil of the mid-century (1840's) Oxford Movement in which General Seminary was thought to be "a hotbed of Tractarian thinking,"[34] he was, as mentioned above, vigilant in the extreme, looking out for any unorthodox practice or thought. By 1870, the related but separate struggles between the high church party and the evangelical wing of the Church and the focus of these struggles in New York and at General Seminary made many wary of the school. Rifts and controversies surrounding the mid-century ecclesiastical trial of New York Bishop Onderdonk and the matter of General graduate Arthur Carey, attacked on grounds of doctrinal unorthodoxy, had still not completely healed.[35] And tensions were further fueled by Onderdonk's own linkage of the early high church movement and the Oxford perspectives. Fairly fanatical vigilance on questions of piety and liturgical practice was the Forbes response.[36] As one commentator puts it, "Forbes' intellectual rigidity and his natural austerity, tinctured now by his antipathy toward Roman Catholicism, led him to believe his greatest service was to root out anything in the Seminary he thought alien to Anglican tradition."[37]

Having joined and then left the Roman Church himself, Forbes was passionate in his bias. He was a zealot in this campaign to such an extreme that he felt it essential to move the Seminary to protect it from these influences. He was supported by those with regional and other biases against New York City's influence within the Church. And he fought bitterly, even by modern standards of academic battles, so much so that Professor Seymour, a key target, eventually reacted by publishing a pamphlet, "A Defence (sic) Against the Assault of the Dean," in which he both responded to Forbes and offered academic and personal attacks of his own on Forbes' leadership.[38]

## *A Lively Neighborhood*

OTHER IMPORTANT ELEMENTS OF THE FORBES CASE for moving the Seminary were provided by the always evolving nature of life in New York City itself, including the lively streets near the Seminary. "Chelsea had long since been engulfed in the expanding sea of traffic and the distracting turmoil of commerce,"[39] wrote Dawley. Significant historical events occurred literally in the midst of the seminarians' lives. For example, the deadly draft riots of 1863 had placed Chelsea at the heart of historic urban stress. During this most lethal public disturbance of the nation's history, Ninth Avenue was taken over by bloodied rioters just a few blocks north of the Seminary and fires and attacks on persons and property occurred throughout the area.[40] Not all of the worldly hubbub was violent. President Lincoln's funeral cortege, on its New York City pilgrimage, made its way up Broadway where a million people jammed the streets, and then passed by the Seminary on its way to the Hudson.

The Seminary's city was dynamic and changing, transformed into one grand building site by the rise of Democratic Party boss William Tweed's Tammany Hall and an explosion of enterprising civic and commercial spirit following the Civil War. Tweed "authorized miles of sewer, water and gas pipelines. Next came roads; by 1873 over a 1,000 men in the pay of the Department of Public Works were laying out miles of hundred-foot-wide macadamized avenues and other narrower streets."[41] The city officially fostered development by leasing or giving away land to hospitals, schools and museums. The Seminary was in the middle of the most vibrant and busy city in the world. The Ninth Avenue elevated train, the only long line on Manhattan, whose "engines belched sparks and inundated pedestrians below with ash," was soon full of workers of all ethnicities moving uptown and

The Ninth Avenue elevated train was a very close and
noisy neighbor for many years.

down between homes and offices, factories and riverfronts. The annual ridership
on New York's thirteen streetcar lines rose to 150 million by 1873.[42] Some of
these trains passed mere feet from the windows of the Seminary.

The riverfront of Chelsea and the entire Lower West Side were profoundly
altered by the construction of the new Grand Central Terminal (begun in 1869),
replacing the previous station on Twenty-Sixth Street. An enormous complex of
grain depots, stockyards and stables arose along the waterfront, just blocks from
the Seminary. Three blocks away in the other direction, large retail establishments
blossomed on Sixth Avenue, "gigantic palaces of consumption," built as "majestic
cast iron frigates" with new-fangled illuminated window displays for Altman's,
Macy's and Stern Brothers, the latter "a two-hundred-foot-wide seven-story
monster" on Twenty-Third Street, just north of the Seminary.[43] The cast-iron

arcades attracted "armies of shoppers, mainly women, promenading and perusing the windows."[44] The area would come to be called "Ladies' Mile."

At the end of the 1860's and early in the 1870's, while Dean Forbes and the Seminary were struggling to pay the bills, the elite and would-be elite of the city were interested in showing off their wealth. "In the affluent fifties they had tilted toward public preening; now in the gilded sixties and seventies, they lurched toward outright ostentation. The adoption of ducal levels of display was driven by tremendous self-assurance—engendered by their victory in war, mastery of peacetime economy and unprecedented accumulation of wealth."[45] In the neighborhood of the Seminary, entertainment impresarios soon followed the retailers. Booth's Theater at Sixth Avenue and Twenty-Third Street offered Shakespeare in a Second Empire temple, but other venues offered simpler fare. One social critic noted "It was getting ever harder to 'violate decency' as the continuing relaxation of standards helped expand the commercial sex industry. After the Civil War, brothels moved north along with the department stores and theaters."[46] Within a few blocks of the Seminary, the so-called Seven Sisters opened seven adjacent brothels in one residential block.

Surrounding the campus Forbes saw urban realities that made him yearn for bucolic Westchester. To the east, Chelsea had become one of the most fashionable quarters in town, rivaled only by the nearby area above Twenty-Third Street to Thirty-Fourth Street and later Fifth Avenue. To the west, danger and sickness bred in the teeming poor neighborhoods along the river. The immigrant residential areas abutting the rail yards, factories and the stinking Manhattan Gas works at Eighteenth and Tenth were foul and violent, with little prospect of uncorrupt police protection.[47] Just a few blocks north of the Seminary, a particularly notorious neighborhood earned the name Hell's Kitchen. In surroundings like these, racial and ethnic tensions as well as labor-owner battles were never far removed. In the hot July of 1871 Irish immigrants, Protestant and Catholic, set off a riot on Eighth Avenue at Twenty-First Street that was only quelled by troops called out from the armories across the city. Sixty were left dead by the tragedy.[48]

## Dean Seymour Accepts the Call

AS VIOLENCE THRIVED IN THE CITY AT LARGE, and dissent divided the Seminary itself, the Board of Trustees took a bold step and forced Forbes out of office in November of 1872. He had insisted for more than a year that he was ready to resign at any time, but supporters kept him at the helm. It took sensational, personal and disparaging arguments, some of which had surfaced during a meeting with students and faculty, to bring him down. Following the Board's decision Morgan Dix recorded in his diary that, with the return of the unwanted parcel of land in Mamaroneck and the resignation of Dean Forbes, two "white elephants thus most happily gotten off of our hands!"[49]

With Forbes' departure, Professor Seymour was named Acting Dean, a position he would hold until 1875 when he accepted the assignment as the full Dean. (The statutes of the Seminary were changed to create a permanent dean, "reversing the former rotary headship" of various faculty that ended with Forbes' term.[50]) Following the Forbes departure, the Board would comment in its traditional Triennial Report:

> The period covered by this report [1869–72] has been marked by excitement and uneasiness, not without their unfortunate results; and to this perhaps are due the rumors and suggestions, generally anonymous and hard to trace to any individual of great evils in the Seminary, of subtle influences at work there perverting the minds of the Students, and of a tendency toward error fostered by the system or its administrators.[51]

Acting Dean Seymour immediately changed course, beginning a new direction, no doubt with the encouragement and support of Dix and Potter and other powerful figures in the New York-centered Church. A new Standing Committee, led by Henry E. Pierrepont, supported "unequivocally the surrender and re-conveyance of the Mamaroneck property."[52] Another committee budgeted funds for immediate use "on the present buildings as may arrest decay and dilapidation."[53] Perhaps symbolically, a long-delayed repair of the painted wooden fence that surrounded the Seminary property was made, with gates installed for access to the neighborhood. Even the Seminary's riverfront wharf and lots were promptly reassessed, then rented to commercial interests.[54]

On the theological front, the Seminary sought to correct explicitly the suggestions put forth by Forbes and his faction that there were Roman or Ritualism influences at work on the Close. "Remembering the Seminary is a general institution, they [the Trustees] desire nothing so much as to banish from it whatever is narrow, local or partisan and to make it reflect the broad light of Catholic truth to all quarters of our common country," the Trustees unanimously announced.[55] Similarly, they sought diplomatically to repair any damage done within ecclesiastical education circles by the rumors of the Forbes era. The Trustees made clear, "The Seminary has no occasion for faulting Diocesan and other Divinity Schools of the Church. She has no heart to bicker and dispute with them. She will pick no quarrel."[56]

Forbes' efforts had, perhaps unintentionally, served to encourage suspicions within these already somewhat divergent educational institutions. The sparks of the Oxford Movement and regional splits between high churchmen and evangelicals were in some ways played out in the nineteenth century through the identities and characters of the individual seminaries of the Episcopal Church. Virginia Theological Seminary had been founded six years after General in 1823 as a regional and evangelical alternative. The Kenyon College theological department led to Bexley Hall in 1824 as a western choice. Later, high church traditionalists trained at General founded three additional seminaries: the Anglo-Catholic seminary at Nashotah House in Wisconsin (1841), Berkeley Divinity School in New Haven (1854) and Seabury in Minnesota (1858). Further, as Episcopal historian Robert Prichard writes, "In 1862, Philadelphia evangelicals, unable to send students to Virginia during the Civil War, formed Philadelphia Divinity School. In 1867, New England evangelicals followed suit, creating the Episcopal Theological School in Cambridge, Massachusetts."[57]

Consequently, acknowledging and promoting the general nature of The General Seminary was profoundly important for its survival. Noting the General Convention's governance and a large Board of Trustees, the Standing Committee reported, "The *Via Media* ["Middle Way"] is secured by the structure of the institution. The Seminary, being in government of the whole Church and every Bishop having visitation powers, is protected against extreme views . . . "[58] A balance was sought and found as the Seminary worked to recover in an enduring way from the tumult of the mid-century. With time, the Chapel of the Good Shepherd would become a centerpiece of this hard-won stability, providing a daily grounding in liturgical practice and priestly formation.

Soon a special committee "For the Development and Improvement of the Seminary" was established, heralding a period of intense change and growth. The Dean Seymour years were vital to the future health of the Seminary. Class size grew, certain grim and disjointed interiors of the East and West Buildings were renovated, which greatly improved the Chapel space in the West Building. The middle way was sought theologically, as well. The general mission of the Seminary was best served by the avoidance of extremes and the establishment of "the moderately Anglo-Catholic devotional tradition characteristic of the student life for many years" subsequent.[59] And with regard to the controversial relationship with the city, Seymour was equally clear: "The location of the Seminary is Salubrious to its proximity to the river and the open space which

surrounds its buildings, admitting a free circulation of air . . . a happy result."[60] He maintained this position throughout his term as dean.

It is remarkable that with all its many accomplishments, Seymour's entire tenure lasted only seven years. When he was consecrated Bishop of Springfield in 1879, he could leave New York knowing that "he had prepared the way for a successor who was to change the face of Chelsea Square" forever.[61] In those seven years he had managed to settle an extraordinarily disruptive period in Seminary life in the city, and in his parting statement he offered a paean to New York. The city, he wrote, "in its influences on the students—broadens the mind, refines the manners and elevates the character. The great city is to the Seminary a Professorial Chair which teaches much and naught else could supply."[62] This understanding of the value of a relationship with New York would be lived out in the Seminary's life for decades to come.

Unfortunately, at the time of his departure the Seminary remained on shaky financial ground, with grossly inadequate facilitates and the continual prospect that intra-church squabbling could once again threaten its presence in Manhattan. An economic blight was partly to blame. From early in 1873 through late 1877 the city and parts of the nation suffered one of the worst economic depressions ever experienced. "New York City's economy fell apart with frightening speed."[63] The real estate bubble burst. Construction projects declined seventy percent between 1871 and 1877. The equities of thousands of property owners, large and small, were wiped away "as with a sponge," as one industry commentator noted.[64] The Seminary's tenants of Hudson River wharf space and the workshop lots on Twenty-First Street failed to pay their much-needed rents.[65] The small merchants and working poor were hurt the most as the city's jobs and incomes evaporated. "The shanty-dwelling population of the West Side burgeoned. Thousands sought shelter on the floors of police stations or almshouses."[66] Charity relief rolls soared. "In 1873 five thousand families had received public assistance; by 1874, twenty-four thousand were being aided."[67] On January 13, 1874 a rally on Tompkins Square "in sympathy with the suffering poor" turned violent, as the police and the city elite showed little empathy for those hurting the most. Class distinctions were on the rise. This all occurred during the chaotic aftermath of the fall of Boss William Tweed, who had defrauded the city of millions and would eventually die in prison.

The four long years of this depression created a complex, precarious and even dangerous climate for a seminary resolutely grappling with its future. Fortunately, the outlook turned for New York and General relatively quickly. The impetus was a recovery program "masterminded by financier and industrialist [and churchman] J.P. Morgan, who'd had enough of extreme financial gyrations."[68] With discipline and clout he set about "managing competition." Under the cloak of devout capitalism, Morgan sought to dramatically dilute the competitiveness of the marketplace. He would eventually achieve nearly complete "Morganization" of the corporate economy through the use of syndicates, trusts, board memberships and financial manipulations. The effects on the city, increasingly the center of American economic life, were profound. Analysts note that, "by 1882 New York was awash in money and power."[69] It had become "a magnet for capital," the "center of the American universe."[70]

## *The Dedicated New Yorker Arrives on the Close*

IT WAS IN THIS CLIMATE that the Board of Trustees elected Eugene Augustus Hoffman as Dean on October 22, 1878. Though the vote was somewhat divided and the new sense of "peace and harmony of the Seminary"[71] remained fragile and the financial and ecclesiastical needs substantial, Hoffman would prove precisely the right choice. Within months he would write to the Board, "In entering upon his duties of The General Theological Seminary, the Dean was at once confronted with a difficult and disabling obstruction growing out of the slender income of the institution."[72] The Seminary spending had been over budget

Eugene Augustus Hoffman. Eastman Johnson, an important artist of the nineteenth century who painted Abraham Lincoln, was Hoffman's portraitist as well.

in each of the previous ten years and expenses often required taking an annual infusion of $8,000 from the slim endowment. Seymour had sheepishly boasted in 1875 that "income had almost equaled expenses"—but for that one year only.[73] Several faculty members took no real salaries and indeed Hoffman's contractual understanding with the Seminary was that as Dean he would be paid "$2,000, annually when such funds were available."

An 1851 graduate of General Seminary, Hoffman arrived fully informed about and prepared to address the school's challenges. A rector for twenty-seven years in New Jersey and New York, he had maintained close ties to his *alma mater*. (Both he and his lawyer-financier father, Samuel Verplanck Hoffmann, served actively on the Standing Committee and the Board of Trustees.)[74] At fifty years of age, the new dean possessed enormous personal wealth and longstanding business connections and friendships. He was part of the New York banking and real estate establishment, his ancestors having arrived in the new world from Amsterdam in the mid-seventeenth century.[75] Hoffman maintained close relations with many of the wealthiest, most privileged families in the city, including the Vanderbilts, the Verplancks, and the Van Cortlandts. His own family fit this mold and his pedigree would prove central to his success at the Seminary.

Hoffman's arrival as Dean coincided perfectly with the end to the mid-1870's economic crisis. While there would be market fluctuations in the period to follow, post-Civil War financial instability had finally come to an end: the Golden Age had begun. The New York historians Burrows and Wallace write in their opus, *Gotham:*

> From 1879 on, frock-coated, silk-hatted brokers jostled and pushed the New York Stock Exchange to new heights. In 1879 [the year of Hoffman's installation] the national and metropolitan markets swung upward again. Reconstruction was over, the South wide open for investment. For the first time in thirty years, New York's bankers, merchants and industrialists faced no significant obstacles to profitmaking.[76]

The commercial sector was creating jobs, which in turn fed a demand for housing and service industries to support the newly employed. The public sector was burgeoning as well, with new bridges, tunnels, rail lines, schools and hospitals. "To meet this demand for housing and commercial space, Manhattan's real estate industry, itself recently organized and housed in a Real Estate Exchange (1883), generated a tremendous amount of commercial construction, much of it now in the red brick Neo-Renaissance style," which was increasingly considered *á la mode*.[77]

The prosperity of the late 70's and early 80's enhanced the prospects of hundreds of families. Mrs. Astor's famous list of "The Four Hundred" socially acceptable now bloomed to a list of two thousand, and with the publication of a new "Social Register," thousands more could climb their way up to an elite status. The old and new money mingled in the marketplace, and "upper-class New Yorkers supported boarding schools, country clubs, exclusive resorts, elite universities and Protestant Church organizations in which blood and money could forge a common culture."[78]

## Shapes Arise

AS THE FACE OF THE CITY CHANGED, so did life in each of its boroughs. Walt Whitman, the devoted New Yorker, was certainly one of the best at capturing the movement and change afoot in his city. [79]

The shapes arise!
Shapes of factories, arsenals, foundries and markets,
Shapes of the two-threaded tracks of railroads,
Shapes of the sleepers of bridges, vast frameworks, girders, arches,
    monuments,
Shapes of the fleets of barges, tows, lake and canal craft, river craft,
Ship-yards and dry-docks and in many a bay and by-place,
The ships themselves on their ways, the tiers of scaffolds, the
    workmen busy outside and inside.

The main shapes rise!
Shapes of Democracy total, result of centuries,
Shapes ever projecting other shapes,
Shapes of the turbulent manly city,
Shapes of the friends and home-givers of the whole earth,
Shapes bracing the earth and braced with the whole earth.

Pulitzer Prize-winning historian David McCullough says that this extraordinary, muscular, risk-taking and dynamic city-building time was the "beginning of heroic

New York." "Think of all of New York of this era as a metaphor for effort!"[80] he proclaims. And what remarkable efforts the island city experienced in the 1880's: the building of the magnificent Brooklyn Bridge (completed only thirty months before the Chapel was started); the construction of the Statue of Liberty in New York harbor, its foundation paid for with the nickels and dimes of the city's school children (the statue, clearly visible from the Chelsea riverfront, was dedicated just weeks before the Chapel's cornerstone was laid); and seminal planning for the Episcopal Cathedral of St. John the Divine (construction would begin while work was underway on the Seminary's Close). "This was a great, founding time for some of the most important, admirable and public institutions," of the city and the nation, asserts McCullough.[81] Carnegie Hall, the Museum of Natural History, the New York Public Library, and the Metropolitan Museum of Art would all open their doors in the 1880's. Historian John Steele Gordon observes that "It was an extraordinary time, with an extraordinary amount of wealth, and there was this notion that one had an obligation to help others and to glorify one's own city."[82] It is in this very climate of effort that Dean Hoffman walked onto the stage of General Seminary and brought with him his own public-spirited energy and dedication to a city and a faith. He was of the same cloth as the bridge and monument builders of his day and of his city—New Yorkers who told the world, "This is built to last, built to stay for all time. We mean business!"[83] On September 4, 1882, three thousand of Thomas Edison's incandescent lamps were lighted downtown: an era of dramatic commitment to growth and technology was underway.

## A Church and a Churchman

THE EPISCOPAL CHURCH WOULD PARTICIPATE IN THE PHENOMENAL GROWTH of wealth in New York, as old-moneyed members thrived and many of the newly wealthy sought the spiritual and social security promised by Church membership. During the same period, the newly rich took an active interest in the performing arts and civic organizations, as well as museums and private schools. Burrows and Wallace's observations are keenly relevant and place Dean Hoffman squarely in the middle of their historical perspective:

> Ecclesiastically speaking, Episcopalians remained the favored denominations of both new and old Protestant elites. Henry Codman

Potter, [Rector of Grace Church] who became Episcopal Bishop of New York in 1887, was pastor to the smart set and had several relatives on Ward McCallister's four hundred list [McCallister was Mrs. Astor's secretary], and when he traveled to church conventions he went in J.P. Morgan's private railroad car. The General Theological Seminary expanded rapidly under Eugene A. Hoffman, its Dean from 1879. Hoffman, descendant of an old Dutch family and owner of real estate worth millions, was said to have been the richest clergyman in the world and was widely known as a sporting parson for his love of hunting and fishing and his active membership in the New York Riding Club.[84]

The Seminary now had as its Dean a man of great means, who was a priest of extraordinary commitment and organizational skill as well. Hoffman was prepared to demonstrate until the very day of his death the seriousness of purpose that the task at General required. And he was prepared to use his personal connections to old money and the aspirations of the newly rich to help create an enduring *general* seminary at the heart of the Church and the heart of the city.

It is apparent that the Seminary "went with him" on a wide variety of adventures along with his prosperous companions. As an active horseman, he took almost daily rides in the fields of northern Manhattan.[85] He also belonged to "what was considered the most exclusive social club in the United States," the Jekyll Island Club on the Georgia coast, which he helped found with the Astors, Vanderbilts, Pulitzers, Morgans and McCormicks.[86] He traveled twice yearly to the Matapedia River, a destination of elite sportsmen, between lower St. Lawrence and the Gaspé region, one of the finest salmon fishing grounds in the world.[87] The funds for his ambitious seminary projects flowed by means of these connections in a way that would not be available to any of his predecessors (or successors). Hoffman was a great fundraiser and, being "of an old New York family, was able to attract less well-connected newly rich New Yorkers who were glad, in association with him, to support the seminary."[88]

His influence within and without the Seminary was apparent each day of his deanship. His biographer noted that from the beginning, "Dr. Hoffman's deanship took on a note of stateliness," as well as confident usefulness.[89] At his very first Board of Trustees meeting on June 5, 1879 he reported that he had spoken with city officials and that the noisome elevated train station on Ninth Avenue had been removed. Further, he met with other residents and merchants in the surrounding area, and the Standing Committee immediately observed that "through the personal influence of the Dean a pride of neighborhood has been aroused, leading residents around the Seminary Square to share in the cost of its good condition and attractive appearance."[90] His detailed correspondence with the Seminary's attorneys shows a willingness to confront the powerful in city government, even on such complex issues as eminent domain claims against the Seminary's valuable Hudson River wharf property.[91]

## Built to Last, Built to Stay

HOFFMAN CAME TO THE SEMINARY AS A BUILDER. He came as a priest and a teacher. While not a theologian, he did articulate a deep understanding of the spiritual basis of his work. His commitment to keeping the Seminary in New York is documented early in his time as Dean. He wrote to his Trustees, "The conviction that . . . the General Institution of the Church . . . should be located in New York has only grown with my experience as Dean. The advantages of giving young men their special training for the ministry in a metropolitan City like this can scarcely be overestimated. A great city is . . . to those who live in it, a kind of University in itself."[92] In this mission he could call upon for support the more than fifty bishops and twelve hundred clergy who were graduates of the seminary at the time.[93]

Hoffman's commitment to the general and non-partisan centrist purpose of the Seminary was expressed again and again. Early on he made a profound commitment: "The Seminary was founded and will be kept . . . as broad and comprehensive as the Church itself."[94] Ever the activist and planner, Hoffman immediately confronted the physical state of the Seminary and called a special meeting in the first weeks of his deanship. He reported, speaking in the third person about himself:

> After conferring with some friends of the Seminary, he determined to gather a few of the most prominent Churchmen of the City and lay its conditions before them. In response to a call signed by the Bishop of New York, the Revs. Dyers, Dix, John Cotton Smith, Morgan and Potter, Messrs. John Cisco, James M. Brown, F. S. Winston, a large meeting composed of gentlemen in financial circles, and representative of various ecclesiastical opinions, was held January 15th [1880] at the office of Mutual Life Insurance Company.[95]

From this meeting would grow the creation of multiple endowments to address the Seminary's needs. The men who convened that day also named a committee of notables to establish an endowment of "at least two hundred and fifty thousand dollars," noting that "more than this will, of course, be required to provide what the Seminary so much needs, additional buildings, a suitable Chapel, a fire-proof library, proper lecture halls, a refectory and more dormitories for Students."[96] (For comparison, it is useful to note that Dean Seymour had proudly pointed to raising $5,300 in a special appeal in his last year.) Hoffman would exceed even his own lofty ambitions. Endowments would be created for professorships, prizes, the Dean's fund and the maintenance of the new buildings.

## The Architect of Choice

DEAN HOFFMAN MADE A SPECIAL PUBLIC ANNOUNCEMENT in 1883 of great significance for the Seminary and all of Chelsea. For the first time he spelled out plans for the construction of a complex of new buildings that would cover the entire block of Seminary land,[97] 200 feet by about 600 feet on Ninth Avenue between Twentieth and Twenty-First Streets. And at its center would be the fine and enduring Chapel that had been needed for more than fifty years.

In contrast to the original twin gray stone structures, the new complex would be constructed of red brick with proper stone trim. The buildings were to be designed by the noted New Yorker, Charles Coolidge Haight, architect of the recently completed buildings at Columbia College. A decorated Civil War veteran and the father of a celebrated cavalryman, Haight's architectural practice received many commissions from family, religious and academic connections.[98]

Of all the buildings that Charles Coolidge Haight designed for the Seminary, it was the Chapel of the Good Shepherd that brought him the greatest satisfaction.

—BERNICE THOMAS

With a genealogy stretching back to early English settlers of the Massachusetts Bay Colony, Haight enjoyed a social and professional status within Episcopalian circles unmatched by any other architect.[99] Indeed, his father, the Rev. Dr. Benjamin Haight had been the well-regarded rector of St. Peter's Church a block away on Twentieth Street, a professor at the Seminary and for many years a priest at Trinity Parish in Wall Street.[100]

Haight's plans called for a careful and ordered arrangement of buildings on the east, west and north edges of the property but left the south open to the city, except for two faculty houses. At the center of the entire property, he envisioned a Chapel that would extend south into the Close, thus creating two linked quadrangles. "The orderliness of the architectural plan was matched by its completeness. Every need of the academic institution was met, including a large dean's residence."[101] The character and the quality of work to be performed were readily apparent to leaders of the Church as well as members of the architectural elite. Morgan Dix, the rector of Trinity Church, Wall Street, said "I know of nothing in the history of collegiate growth and expansion to equal this."[102] The first great New York architecture critic, Montgomery Schuyler, called the Seminary a "brilliant success" and referred to it as "Haight's masterpiece."[103] In 1917 Haight's *Architectural Record* obituary would refer to his work at the Seminary as some of "the very best of his time," and the Chapel as "reflecting the lofty dignity" of the city at its best.[104]

The preparations for the formal laying of the cornerstone of the Chapel in June 1886 forced Forbes-era battlers such as Bishop Arthur Cleveland Coxe of the Diocese of Western New York to acknowledge that they had lost the war. "[T]he building of a Chapel on the Seminary grounds is about to begin. This is the equivalent to saying that the Seminary is condemned for all time to occupy . . . a city very rapidly losing every quality."[105] While Hoffman and Haight would concur that the building of the Chapel set in stone their commitment to a relationship with New York, they would see the qualities that the city offered very differently.

Charles Coolidge Haight was a special advocate of the English Gothic Revival Movement, which he used and adapted to collegiate and ecclesiological architecture. This movement originated in the eighteenth century and culminated in the nineteenth; it sought to revive the spirit and forms of Gothic architecture in public, residential, educational and religious settings. There was in this style an enthusiastic acceptance of the English church form, particularly in its Gothic iteration, by high church Episcopal leaders in America.[106] Haight also pioneered the use of the English university quadrangular campus plan, not widely used in America until the twentieth century.[107] Haight experimented with this quadrangular layout first at Columbia College's original campus and then at the Seminary, which "is the oldest example of this arrangement still extant in New York."[108] In addition to his commissions at Columbia and the Seminary, Haight designed a significant quadrangle of buildings at Yale University, numerous Fifth Avenue mansions and, later, The Church of St. Ignatius of Antioch[109] and the Trinity School in Manhattan, whose board was chaired by Dean Hoffman. Hoffman and Haight took inspiration from Magdalen College at Oxford, England. A visual and textual review of the design of Magdalen College readily reveals the comparison, particularly in the tower design.[110]

## The Grand Design

THE NEW PLAN CALLED FOR AN ORDERLY ARRANGEMENT OF STRUCTURES on the Seminary land. With all the buildings except the Chapel kept to the periphery, Hoffman observed that the "function of the grounds as a park is interfered with as little as possible."[111] The thoughtful order of the plan was enhanced by its completeness. Haight had addressed every need of the "learned institution," and the ambitious undertaking was referred to as Hoffman's "grand design."[112] When

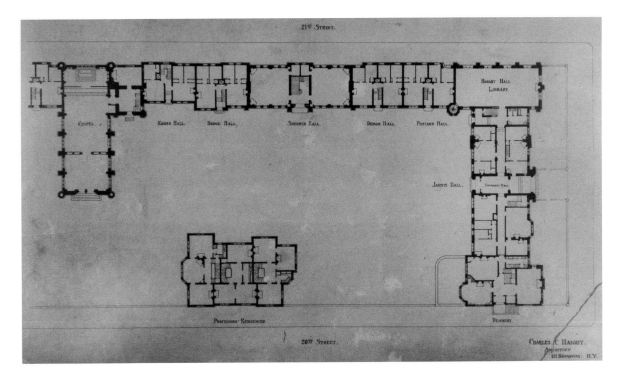

construction was finally finished in 1904, the new seminary was almost exactly as he envisioned it nineteen years earlier. Between 1884 and 1904 Haight completed sixteen buildings for the Seminary in fulfillment of Hoffman's master plan: Sherred Hall (1883–84); Dehon Hall (1885); Pintard Hall (1885); The Chapel of the Good Shepherd, cornerstone laid June 16, 1886 (1886–88); Kohne Hall (1891); Dodge Hall (1891); Chelsea 2/3/4 (1892); Chelsea 8/9 (1897); Jarvis Hall (1887, later demolished and replaced); Hobart Hall (1895, later demolished and replaced); The Deanery (1885, later demolished and replaced); Hoffman Hall (1889–1900); Eigenbrodt Hall (1899–1900); Lorillard Hall (1902–03); White Hall (1902–03); Edson Hall (1902–03).[113]

As any regular visitor to the existing campus knows, constantly changing patterns of light and shadow bathe the south-facing Close. The arrangement of the buildings, their materials and composition contribute to a surprising and even magical effect. The general impression is one of coherence and permanence, achieved through the use of homogenous materials and careful scale and massing, interrupted only by the tower of the Chapel. Critics have noted, "It was very straightforward work in which Haight relied for effect upon the disposition of the buildings and in which the decoration was always an outward and visible expression of the underlying construction."[114] Haight's interpretation of the Collegiate Gothic Revival established him as one of its pioneers. Schuyler wrote a long assessment of Haight's work in which he concluded that a "sense of appropriateness" was the mark of his great talent. "It is of no school. It is a personal quality."[115]

## The Indefatigable Builder Calls on a Few Friends

IN REALIZING THIS EXTRAORDINARY ENDEAVOR Eugene Hoffman wanted to engage many of the finest artisans in the country, so he drew upon the resources of some of the wealthiest Episcopalians to help him. Undaunted by the scale of his task, Dean Hoffman set to work raising funds for his financially secure, moderate, disciplined and urban *general* seminary. He used all of the financial, social and church connections he could muster, and historical documents bear testament to his success with familiar signatures on appeals, an impressive roster of donors, the employment of the finest artisans, and the widespread endorsement by the architectural elite and the New York press. His lengthy 1882 case for funds was co-signed or supported by Horatio Potter, the Bishop of New York, rectors

THE INDEFATIGABLE BUILDER CALLS ON A FEW FRIENDS

Dix of Trinity Church, Potter of Grace Church, Morgan of St. Thomas Church, Tiffany of Zion Church, Henry Pierrepont and Cornelius Vanderbilt. The appeal was featured in *The Churchman*[116] and more than $100,000 quickly raised. The Dean's mother became a major donor with her contribution of $150,000 for the Chapel, in memory of her late husband, Samuel Verplanck Hoffman. Other family gifts would regularly follow, including many from Hoffman himself—though his are frequently hard to trace. As Dawley notes, "The full amount of Hoffman's personal munificence will never be known, for there are many gifts noted as coming 'through the Dean' or 'from a friend.' Such phrases often concealed the generosity of Eugene Augustus Hoffman."[117]

Comfortable avoiding extremes while maintaining his standard high churchmanship, and not about to be distracted by partisan debates, Eugene Hoffman was an indefatigable builder, and according to Bernice Thomas, the noted architectural writer, "had been one long before he began his grand design at the Seminary."[118] At each of the New York, New Jersey and Pennsylvania parishes in which he served, Hoffman presented vestries with building plans and proposals, many of which were pursued. Using his owns funds as seed money to inspire others (a pattern he followed at General), Hoffman built parish houses, new churches, schools and rectories. While serving as the dean of the Seminary, he was also chairman of the board of Trinity School and responsible for its move to the West side and a campus of handsome new buildings.[119] His work as the first Chairman of the Building Committee of the Cathedral of St. John the Divine is commemorated by an honorific column in the sanctuary, which stands next to John Jacob Astor's. His appeal for funds for the Seminary reads like an inspired banker's prospectus. He reviews in great detail the status of the institution, the value and sources of its funding, the personnel and faculty strengths, needs and changes, and the prospects for success. He does all this while emphasizing the fundamental mission of the Seminary in New York. And he describes the recent past as "the [destructive] excitement . . . created by the unfortunate party spirit . . . aroused in those days, of which the Seminary was too often made the battleground." He concludes bluntly: "It is a marvel that its doors were not closed."[120]

From Twenty-First Street looking south: the Seminary and the city beyond; a nearby gasworks' tower marks the river. Lithograph: J. Evers, 1841.

Hoffman clearly understood the importance of his grand scheme. His plan, with the Chapel as its centerpiece, would establish a seminary for the Church at large, a church alive in the city and in the world. He called for the Seminary in all things to hold to an "even and moderate course, through agitations and panic." In his call for an endowment to maintain and firmly re-establish a seminary "as broad and comprehensive as the Church itself," he did not shy away from blunt threats: Without new and substantial support, he wrote, "no prophet is needed" to see "not only gradual decline, but ultimate disaster."

Eugene Hoffman had no intention of presiding over a disaster of any sort. On the contrary, as his biographer Theodore Riley asserts, "He had come into this work with a certain great joy. He had known the ordinary life of the Church to its fullest extent and now he saw how he could energize and beautify a larger sphere within the Church . . . He had come out of large pastoral experience; he had come back to his *alma mater*, whose necessities and whose possibilities with his statesmanlike vision he perfectly saw."[121] Hoffman secured public notice of his intentions in frequent press reports. As Riley notes, "Almost every prominent journal of the day paid tribute to the work he had at once taken in hand."[122] *The New York Times* of June 28th, 1880 editorialized, "The movement to place the General Theological Seminary of the Episcopal Church on a level with the strongest schools in the country, and enlarge its range of instruction and its inclusion of schools of opinion, is a laudable and notable sign of the times."[123]

## Kindred Spirits

CLEARLY, HOFFMAN HAD FOUND A KINDRED SPIRIT IN HAIGHT, but he also must have seen a creative genius with access to the most talented artisans and a visionary with clear understanding of the prevailing aspirations for superb public architecture. The partners seemed to be in near total agreement on many design questions and Hoffmann would later collaborate with Haight on projects elsewhere in the city, including Trinity School and Hoffman Hall at the New York Yacht Club where they were both active members. Bernice Thomas suggests "an intimate partnership between architect and patron."[124]

"Of all the buildings that Haight designed for the Seminary, it was the Chapel of the Good Shepherd that brought him the greatest satisfaction . . ." she writes.[125] Following its grand dedication in 1888, Haight would read in *The New York Times,* under a headline "Magnificent Gift," that "Two hundred white-robed clergymen solemnly dedicated yesterday morning one of the most beautiful chapels in the country."[126] *The Brick Builder,* an architecture and building professional journal would note that, "The seminary Chapel's entrance, facing south for warmth, sunlight and welcome to those outside, serves to divide and shape the traditional English quadrangle, providing also contrasted height and character of building."[127] With its large pointed arch windows, the exterior lengths of the Chapel are articulated with brick buttresses marking each bay. The red brick, most likely made in Hudson River towns such as Haverstraw or Croton, is supported on a base of rusticated brownstone quarried at Belleville, New Jersey. A dark slate roof provides a stately and secure appearance.

## Through the Gates into the City

AS ANY VISITOR CAN SEE, THE CHAPEL'S PORTAL FACES THE CITY rather than the main entrance of the Seminary, a design customary at the time. As contemporary architect and expert on the Seminary's design, Samuel White suggests, "They [Hoffman and Haight] seemed to expect that an important focus and view of

the entire Seminary would be from the city, the world outside."[128] This is an architectural embodiment of a fundamental idea. The top step inscription, stepped over and barely noticed by so many who visit the Chapel, also reinforces this idea. It reads, "Blessed are they that enter in through the gates into the City."[129] This is adapted from the closing chapter in the apocalyptic New Testament Book of Revelation. It is a prophecy that points to a particular city, "as beautiful as a precious jewel built on foundation walls bearing the names of the Apostles," the New Testament scholar Raymond Brown notes.[130] This is a metaphor for the New Jerusalem: a holy city where God's purposes and human life are in total harmony. Hoffman inscribed this quotation on the broad welcoming step so that everyone moving into or going out of his chapel would pass over a powerful reminder of the invitation both to inhabit a future heavenly city and to work for God's purposes in the human city as well.

## Creating Treasures with Talent

KEY FEATURES OF THE ENTRANCE are the magnificent bronze doors, vesica and tympanum above. The doors, lauded by critics, depict particularly vivid scenes from the life of Christ. Several of the scenes focus on discipleship. As so many chapel-goers are rushing in to services at the very last moment, these amazing works of art are often not given the careful attention they deserve.[131] Hoffman and Haight selected a young Scottish immigrant, J. Massey Rhind, who had trained at the Royal Academy in Edinburgh, to sculpt the doors, tympanum and vesica, which were later cast by John Williams Company of New York, one of several renowned firms that made New York a key center for bronze casting.[132] The tympanum was a common form of early door head "combining an arch with a lintel for strength," the resultant space above was a popular site for sculpture.[133] The relief over the door was Rhind's first commission in America and was modeled from an engraving chosen by Hoffman himself. He completed it in memory of Hoffman's oldest son (also named Eugene), who died at the age of twenty-eight. Young Eugene is memorialized in a text above the door frame that includes the family crest.

Dean Hoffman could clearly identify great talent, and Rhind would come to be one of the foremost American sculptors of his era.[134] The breathtaking beauty of his Chapel doors stems in part from their accessible narrative power. They tell wonderful, familiar stories with images of figures and locations that ring true with an inviting and warm character. The doors were most likely cast

from terra cotta sculptures. This is a medium that permits the high relief, carefully finished modeling, and subtle detail that is clearly present. All of the figures Rhind created display visible tool marks and shadings, suggesting enormous care. The figures are sturdy and active and move out from their Gothic-style scroll pattern borders of leaves and grapes into a clearly three-dimensional space, closer to the viewer. Many figures have had deep undercutting that makes them appear particularly alive and full of character. Distinctive individual personalities, body types and personal expressions are powerfully present. The foot of Peter, kneeling before Jesus on one panel, has become shiny and worn by the frequent touch of many students' hands, not unlike the similar touch given to Peter's sculpted foot by countless visitors to the Vatican basilica in Rome. Perhaps most notably, the depiction of Jesus as the Good Shepherd (with two somewhat scrawny lambs) sets a tone of calm confidence, clarity and purposefulness in ministry, an image that

generations of seminarians have walked under each of their days at General. Both the bronze doors and the reredos figures were part of the original plan, but not realized for more than a decade after the Chapel opened.

Following Rhind's work at the Seminary, his New York opportunities grew and his next commission consisted of bronze doors for Trinity Church.[135] (They formed part of a memorial for John Jacob Astor III.) Success followed success and Rhind gradually became a celebrated sculptor noted for civic, ecclesiastical and society art works, including a number of important World War I memorials.[136] The use of bronze for major sculptural works was a relatively new development in the fine arts in America. In the 1850's, "bronze casting in the United States had taken on added symbolism as a medium that reflected America's growing confidence and ambition."[137] Rhind received commissions from the Carnegie family for works that appear in many Carnegie libraries, as well as the Carnegie Institute in Pittsburgh. Today, his heroic and commemorative sculpture still graces public and private buildings and monuments throughout the United States and Canada, including the U. S. Capitol, Princeton University, the Federal Building in Providence and the World War I Memorial in Halifax.

OPPOSITE: The Roosevelt organ, the side pulpit, and the brass gates, all features of the original Chapel design, now lost.

## A Sacred Space

AFTER PASSING THROUGH RHIND'S DOORS and entering the Chapel, one is immediately made aware of the seriousness of purpose that Hoffman demanded throughout. This was and remains a Chapel for the Church at large, a Chapel for the formation of leaders, a Chapel for the city and the world. The fine craftsmanship demonstrated in every element is readily apparent. A review of photographs of the Gothic Revival Keble College, Oxford confirms the similarities of the two chapels, strongly suggesting Hoffman's bias toward the lasting Anglican traditions as interpreted through the Catholic revival.[138] The interior of the Chapel of the Good Shepherd is a deep rectangular space, but with a complexity and richness that belies the initial simplicity. A visitor is immediately struck by the high vaulted ceiling of carefully carved and arched chestnut beams, ribs and brackets, with amply decorated spandrels. The master carpenters' skills are also evident. And one's eye is drawn to the altar with the towering reredos behind, dramatically lighted in present times.

Enormous care has been taken with this interior, and a study of the original architectural drawings in the Archives of the Seminary reveals that Haight personally inspected and changed scores of details.[139] The drawings for the oak rood screen show the precise scoring and dimensions required. Carved in New York oak by the architectural sculptors Ellis and Kitson, the screen is considered a rare and fine example, called at the time (perhaps a bit too enthusiastically) "without doubt the most effective and beautiful piece of carved oaken work in this country."[140] Ellis and Kitson were also known for exquisite work at Grace Church on Broadway and such projects as the interior of the Vanderbilt home in Newport.

Rood screens, topped with a rood (a carved figure of the crucified Christ), were a common feature in late Gothic church architecture, and are both physical and symbolic barriers. They separate the chancel and sanctuary—the traditional places of the clergy—from the nave where the people would congregate and worship. During the late Medieval period, "joinery skill reached its zenith, resulting in a wealth of stall work and screen with which both greater and lesser parish churches were well supplied."[141] These screens were a major target of the Reformation desire to remove venerated or worshiped images, and hardly any Medieval rood screens remain in Britain.

In academic chapels the rood screen traditionally divided the academic community from guests and family. Such was the situation at the Seminary,

where for many generations the screen also included a brass gate in the center aisle that divided the ante-chapel worshipers from those in the main chapel. The smaller ante-chapel has traditional altar-facing seats and was to be used by family members, visitors and latecomers. In the twentieth century the gate was removed, and in contemporary times guests are most welcome to sit in the choir with students.

The Chapel's screen has no rood, but is topped by an elaborately carved cross of oak and six standing, exuberant angels each with a musical instrument.[142] As in English collegiate chapels, such as Keble and Magdalen in Oxford, much of the interior space is in front of the rood screen and is set in antiphonal or choir formation (one side's pews facing the other side's) with elaborately carved wooden stalls, students on the lower tiers and dean and sub-dean and faculty on the upper tier. The deans' stalls are canopied in the same carved oak. For many generations, although no longer, the students sat in rank order with senior students just below the faculty. The choir-wise arrangement permits and encourages the antiphonal singing of the daily Offices, and facilitates the ceremonial traditions that Hoffman nurtured. On several faculty stalls, the old names of the professorial chairs, no longer used according to their designations, are still faintly lettered in gold.

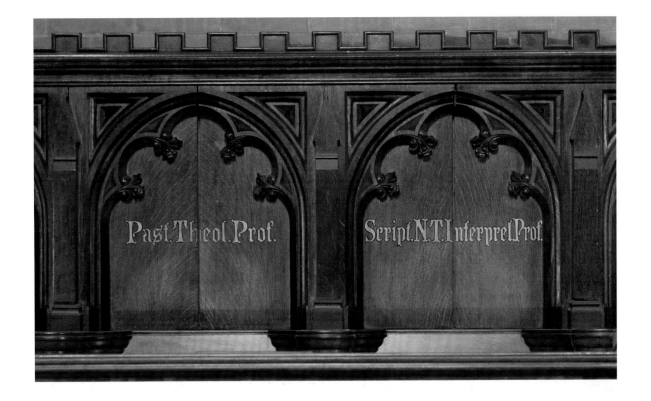

## Stones with Purpose

THE PROFOUNDLY SERIOUS NATURE OF THE SEMINARY'S UNDERTAKING and its ancient roots are never far away in this sacred space. Over the stalls, carved in stone and inlaid with gold leaf, appears the Latin 1662 version of the English consecration prayer for the ordination of priests, a formula adapted from the medieval Sarum Rite of the Salisbury Cathedral, which includes "be thou a faithful dispenser of the word of God." The interior walls are of fine Roman brick in contrasting shades of deep red and pale yellow, a design clearly drawn from the Keble College interior and exterior brickwork. The design in the brickwork echoes the lower arches in the wooden stalls and the stonework in the sanctuary.

This and all the stonework throughout the Chapel is exquisite. Above the altar the Greek letters symbolizing Christ, the *Alpha* and *Omega* and the *Chi Rho* appear in the stone. A Greek cross graces the north wall.[143] The floors of the Chapel are a precisely laid mosaic in Parisian stones. Down the center aisle quatrefoil designs frame the cardinal and the holy virtues and across the front the theological virtues called for by Paul in his first letter to the Corinthians.[144] One of Haight's remarkably detailed corrective notes on the original plans directs that the Latin words for the virtues be written on a straight line, not an arc. It has been suggested that "the marble mosaic pavement provides a rose red carpet that unfolds down the nave, a continuous progression of more than one hundred feet toward the altar."[145] Another historian referred to this elegant catechetical feature as inspiration itself, creating a "sermon in stone."[146]

## A Chapel with a Mission

Many of the distinctive marks of academic and community custom at the General Seminary owe their origin to regulations or practices instituted by Eugene Hoffman. [He] was determined, by precept and example, to make the chapel the vital center of the common life of Chelsea Square, and his success in establishing this tradition is where the Seminary's lasting indebtedness to him lies.[147]

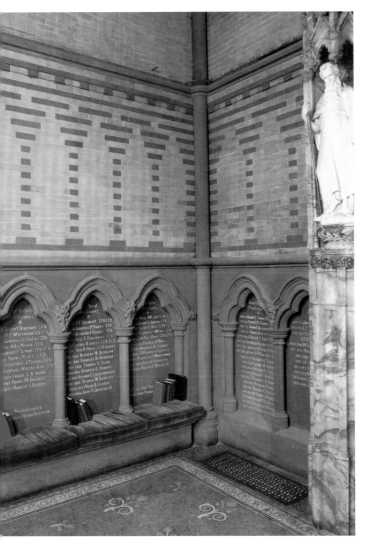

This is manifested in the remarkably detailed *Digest of the Rules and Regulations of the Seminary relating to The Students, compiled for their use by The Dean*.[148] This document was considered a "second Bible"[149] by some students, and in its various editions Hoffmann portrayed the devout gentleman-scholar he expected the General seminarian to be. The rules began with the "Matriculation Vow," crafted by Hoffman himself, "to be signed by every student on his admission to the Seminary." Signatures were provided on All Saints' Day initially under the eye of the Registrar in the Tower Room and then later under the gaze of the Dean and Faculty assembled as part of a distinctive annual service in the Chapel. This vow committed each new student "to cultivate religious and moral dispositions and habits." Each year's Matriculation service in the Chapel remains an important moment in the life of seminarians and an opportunity for the community to welcome new students as they begin their formation for ministry.

Hoffman's regulations at that time called for compulsory attendance at daily Morning and Evening Prayer services and at the Holy Eucharist celebrated on Sundays, Thursdays and Holy Days. Further, the spiritual direction of each student was to fall "under the Dean and no one else." Students were required to wear academic gowns and to sit within the rood screen. If not gowned or found sitting in the nave, they would be counted absent. Attendance was taken at each service and "irregularity in attendance . . . brought to the attention of the Bishop to whose Diocese the student belongs." All students were required to attend Matriculation, the Commencement sermon and Commencement services. Graduation could be denied if this rule was violated. These were new customs for students and faculty alike, and by this extraordinary rigidity Dean Hoffman hoped to instill a "seriousness" and the "pious and studious habits, which become persons preparing for the Holy Ministry." Hoffman also gave fastidious attention

to the smallest details in the care of the Chapel. A memo in his own hand calls for daily dusting of the nave and the weekly washing of windows in the sacristy "inside and out."[150] This was not mere fussiness; the Chapel meant a great deal to him. "It meant first the daily approach to God, the source of daily light and health. It meant companionship in prayer of his brethren of the faculty . . . and of the dear youth, his sons in the seminary fold."[151]

The Chapel of the Good Shepherd stood at the heart of Dean Hoffman's plan and became the heart of student life, the source of community identity and of religious practice. Hoffman hoped that, with its "central commanding position . . . it will daily remind students that far above the education of the library and the lecture room, there is spiritual preparation needed for the priests of the Church."[152] Seminarians who have attended General have consistently experienced chapel life as a foundational feature of their formation for ministry. From the earliest days of the Seminary, students have been participants at each service and have sung the daily Offices. Soon after the Chapel of the Good Shepherd was consecrated, a commentator noted:

> The Chapel is the very center of the life in the seminary. The effect of daily and evening prayers and the frequent celebrations of the Holy Eucharist on the spiritual life of the students is deep and lasting, fitting them more than all the other influences of the seminary for the holy work of ministry.[153]

## The Sacristans and The Precentors

FOR MANY GENERATIONS a guild of student Sacristans has opened, organized, cleaned and prepared the Chapel for services. Similarly, student Precentors have led the community in musical worship, and student Chimers have called them to prayer. In the twentieth century these were organized as formal guilds with elections for Chiefs and a detailed Rota. The tradition of Sacristans is an ancient one, related to the duties of the sexton. A description of the nineteenth century Anglican sacristan, which Hoffman would have known, notes that "he is found three hundred and fifty evenings in the year, moving about the sacristy and the sanctuary with loving devotion, laying out vestments, replacing candles, filling cruets, changing linens that all may be celebrated with cleanliness and godly fear on the morrow."[154] For the seminarians at General Seminary, at least from Hoffman's time, a similar, if more modern, attitude of great care is taken by the Guild of Sacristans. Each member makes a voluntary commitment of many hours of labor led by a Chief who today is responsible for over twenty services each

OPPOSITE: For more than a generation the voices of the
Schola Cantorum have graced the community.

week, far exceeding almost any church, seminary, or even many cathedrals. An early twentieth century guide, "The Sacristan's Manual" calls for a guild of twelve members to carefully divide their labors around such tasks as altar preparation, cleaning of the silver vessels and the care of linen, as well as the preparation for the various liturgies and welcoming Chapel guests.[155] The process for selection and responsibilities of the Guild of Sacristans has evolved over the years, but all members remain engaged in a dedicated ministry to the community that is essential for the daily life of the Chapel.

Similarly, a Guild of Precentors has served the community musically. Precentors, from the Latin word *praecentor,* meaning first singer, are students who have taken responsibility for leading the community in chanted prayer and song. Two years after the consecration of the Chapel, a long article in the national periodical *The Illustrated American* reported on General Seminary life in detail and noted, "The music is extraordinarily beautiful, wholly Gregorian and is rendered and led by the students, with only the organ to help sustain their remarkable voices . . . music not surpassed by that of any chapel of Cambridge or Oxford."[156] Until the 1950's participation in choral music was required of all students, and rehearsals were built into the Seminary schedule.[157] This is no longer the case. However, the legacy of featuring the daily Offices musically and liturgically has continued. The Guild of Precentors, with music faculty guidance, has become even more essential to Chapel worship, as the general student body has little time for musical rehearsal. The Precentors serve as prompters for congregational singing as well as leaders and supporters of liturgical continuity in each service of Office and, over time, in the general music offering of the Chapel. David J. Hurd, the longtime Professor of Church Music and Organist of the Chapel notes that because of the commitment of the Precentors, Chapel worshippers have been able to participate regularly in "fine settings of Morning Prayer and Evening Prayer by major composers."[158] He says, "The Precentors are the force that cements continuity in the Chapel music program." In 1976 Hurd restored group choral music with the creation of The Schola Cantorum, a group of students who sing choral works at community Eucharists and in recital.

## *Remarkable Instruments*

ON OCTOBER 31, 1888 AT THE CONSECRATION OF THE CHAPEL, it was "filled with a quality and volume of sacred song which had rarely if ever been equaled at any service this side of the Atlantic."[159] Since that day when the organ played Luther's great chorale, "A mighty fortress is our God," organ music has shaped and greatly enhanced the voices of students, faculty and guests in the celebration of daily Chapel life.

As he did with each of the craftsmen deployed to create the Chapel, Hoffman chose an esteemed and admired artisan to build the organ. Hilborne Roosevelt was "considered the best known [American] organ builder, effecting many bold improvements" in the traditional church instrument.[160] Like many of those Hoffman

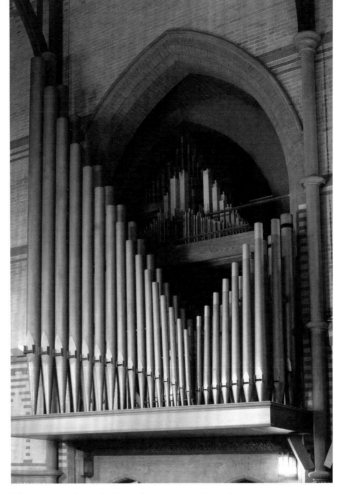

commissioned, Roosevelt enjoyed lofty social and church connections; he was a first cousin of Theodore Roosevelt and a close personal friend of Thomas Edison. Having built the organ for the nation's centennial exhibit at the 1876 World's Fair, as well as other significant church organs including those of Trinity Church in Boston and First Presbyterian in Manhattan, Hilborne Roosevelt was a natural choice. One of his fine organs could also be enjoyed just a half-block away at St. Peter's Episcopal Church on Twentieth Street, where Haight's father had been rector. The Roosevelt organ in the Chapel was commissioned in 1886 and installed as the Chapel was finished. (Hilborne Roosevelt died suddenly during this work at the age of 36, but his brother Frank and the Roosevelt Organworks of eight skilled craftsmen carried on.) While the exact specifications of the organ are no longer available, it was a "tracker-pneumatic" organ assisted by Barker levers in all divisions. The "tracker action" in such organs is described as, "a very simple yet painstakingly precise system of rods and levers which connected the organist's finger (or foot) to a valve at the end of each pipe." [161]

The hundreds of pipes of the Chapel's Roosevelt Opus 385 were housed in the pipe chamber on the second floor of the tower, which opened into the chapel at the liturgical south side (to the right facing the altar). The unscreened pipes were flush with the wall. The keyboard was immediately beneath the pipes in the area of the choir where the Sacristans sit today. For more than seventy years this organ accompanied the chant for daily Offices, and the singing of hymns and choral performances. It was an excellent organ, but thought by some to be somewhat deep and muddied in tone, and with its pipes recessed in the second floor chamber, some fading away of notes occurred.

In 1958, during the dynamic deanship of Lawrence Rose, the present organ was installed in the Chapel. It was dedicated to the teaching and ministry of much-loved Chaplain and Greek teacher, Miles Lowell Yates, "a priest of wide pastoral experience, counselor and confessor to students and faculty alike" during the years of World War II and following.[162] Designed and built by Walter Holtkamp of Cleveland, this powerful instrument is of the "American neo-baroque" style and is considerably larger, with a "brighter and more sparkling sound," than the Roosevelt.[163] Many of its pipes were brought out of the pipe chamber into the Chapel itself and rest on a large shelf, which projects above the arched doorway to the Tower Room.

In 1959, Carl Weinrich, recognized at the time as, "one of the greatest living performers of Bach's organ music," made an RCA Victor recording of several Bach fugues and toccatas in the Chapel on the new Holtkamp organ.[164] In an essay on the Seminary's organ, he observed:

> The sound is rich and satisfying, projected directly into the nave. Since there is no gallery, the Positiv pipes, which normally would be placed on the gallery wall behind the organ bench, are located in front of the Great division. The large pedal pipes, which are often in the rear, occupy the front and most conspicuous position, making them particularly effective in sound and prompt in speech. The instrument is eminently suitable for the performance of the great organ music of Bach.[165]

He also applauded the fact that the Chapel interior "is entirely without acoustic treatment and thus has the reverberation most desirable for organ tone." Given the electrical action of the Holtkamp organ, greater flexibility was permitted in the placement of its keyboard which sits on the main floor of the Chapel and has wheels that permit the organist at any time to turn and face the choir, congregation or accompanists as desired.

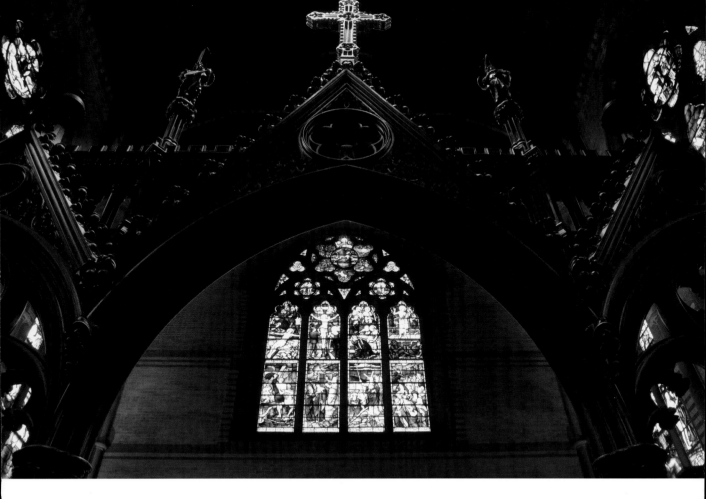

## Transparently Beautiful

A DETAILED STUDY OF THE EXTRAORDINARY STAINED GLASS WINDOWS of the Chapel was completed by Peter D. D'Angio in 1994.[166] He notes that however familiar the surroundings of the Chapel become to daily visitors, "one thing that continues to draw our attention and lifts us out of our sense of indifference is the windows."[167] It is almost certain that Dean Hoffman was intimately involved in the details of these centrally important features. He had shown a keen interest in the quality of stain glass windows in each of the parishes where he served as rector.[168] D'Angio concludes that John Henry Hopkins, Jr., a New York cleric and 1850 graduate of the Seminary and later a voice instructor, organist and composer, selected the subjects of the panels under Hoffman's direction. (The announcement published by the Seminary on the occasion of the consecration of the Chapel credits Hopkins.[169]) He was the son of John Henry Hopkins, Sr., who was the first Bishop of Vermont, in 1865 chosen the Presiding Bishop. Hopkins, Sr.

was an accomplished painter and writer, interests and skills he passed along to his son. The windows were designed and created by the London firm of Lavers, Barraud and Westlake, a world-renowned workshop considered to be at the peak of the craft. As Bernice Thomas notes, the Chapel is greatly enhanced by their remarkable workmanship, "so much more unity and more color are introduced by a full program of stained glass windows."[170] It is likely the designer of the windows was Nathaniel Westlake himself, as he was handling the design on major commissions during the 1880's.[171] He was a scholar, an artist, and a fellow at the British Museum, which published a number of his drawings and plans.[172] So-called "Antique glass" was used by designers of this period. The material is thicker and has more texture than ordinary glass; thus the glass itself creates much of the visual interest.[173]

The scale of the undertaking is obvious. There are ninety-one separate Biblical scenes in the ten windows of the Chapel with each scene making up one panel of

a window. Panel by panel, D'Angio carefully described the Biblical stories depicted. He notes that there are some duplications and some textual oddities. There is an explicit scriptural reference (or multiple references in the case of Gospel stories) on each panel of each window. Further, there is a clear scheme of "typology" used in the windows. This means that a correspondence has been created between the top two or three panels of each vertical frame of each window, which typically refers to New Testament passages, and the lower one with an Old Testament depiction. "The custom in Biblical illustration [became] for Old Testament 'types' to be juxtaposed with New Testament 'antitypes,' to demonstrate visually that the promise of the Old Testament was fulfilled in the New."[174]

An ideal example of this arrangement is provided by the fourth window on the liturgical north side of the Chapel.[175] It is topped with a relatively small depiction of Luke's account (5:1–11) of the miraculous catch of fish, one of the first scenes of Jesus calling his disciples. The colors in the image are bright, the fish dramatic, and the surprise of Peter, James and John quite apparent as they visibly strain in the water under their bountiful load. This small rose window sets the theme for the entire window: the preparation for God's presence and action in human life. Water (or water-related images, such as flood, fish, baptism and rainbows) are the mediators of the action.

Specifically, in the Old Testament image below, as D'Angio notes, "Westlake gives us a glimpse of what he imagines the building of the ark must have been like."[176] Again, the figures are strong and crisp, with Medieval costume and tools. The flood is coming and the ark, a metaphor for the church, is being built. Above, John, the one who baptizes with water, opens his mouth to speak to the crowd below him, "yet he speaks directly out into the space of the Chapel, as if we are part of the crowd," D'Angio observes. John the Baptist's hand-held banner reads, *Para . . . via Domini,* "Prepare the way of the Lord," the words of Isaiah that John uses in both Matthew (3:3) and Mark (1:3). Above, preparation is indeed underway in a panel on Church building, a powerful theme in the lives of Hoffman and Haight who, as did many ecclesiastical builders, inserted their own presence into their project. Indeed, D'Angio suggests that the Gothic figure in this panel consulting the plans could well be Westlake himself.[177] It could also be a reference to the work underway at the Seminary.

The most powerful panel in this window is the lower-center depiction of the ark floating in the storm, from Genesis (7:17). With crackling lightning above and the house-like ark floating below, the panel features two large fish not unlike the plump salmon Hoffman is known to have caught on his excursions in Canada. This viewer can see his influence in the exciting image of outdoor adventure and God's constant presence. D'Angio notes that Westlake uses the fish image or the fish-like shape in many of the panels where God breaks into the human story. Citing the theologian Canon Edward West, he suggests that these shapes are used to "indicate visually the entry of God into the earthly realm."[178] The top and bottom right panels each contain rainbow images: first as the sign of the covenant that God made with Noah representing the Old Testament type, then as the depiction from the Book of Revelation of Christ surrounded by a rainbow of colored cherubim as the New Testament antitype (4:3).

Together the window panels present a complex, sophisticated and masterfully executed effort to bring scripture and faith alive in the minds and hearts of worshipers in the Chapel. The power of these particular windows is their capacity to speak to us and to draw us into their vivid stories. Each window presents a similarly powerful mix of symbols and narrative. One further iteration of this is the handsome border depicting a grapevine that divides upper and lower window panels. This internal tracery forms a ribbon, which wraps around the interior of the Chapel and continues outside on the buildings of the Close. Organic and subtle, it stands as a potent reminder of the centrality of the Eucharist with its sacramental wine in Hoffman's grand design.[179]

## Changing Life around the Altar

FOR ALMOST ONE HUNDRED AND TWENTY YEARS the Eucharist has been celebrated at the altar of the Chapel. This altar is far more than a table; it is also a work of sacred art. The altar now stands atop broad steps of gray Italian marble. The altar itself is of marble, rose alabaster, and Caen stone. It was created by the New York stone design firm of Fischer and Bros.

In the summer of 1968, under the direction of the new dean, Samuel Wylie, the New York architectural restoration firm of Moore and Hutchins was retained

The oldest known interior photograph, prior to the 1897 electric lights,
the 1906 pulpit and long before the altar was moved forward.

to design and complete a major alteration of the altar and sanctuary. The altar was taken down from its high position against the wall and moved out seven feet into the sanctuary to permit the celebrant of the Eucharist to stand behind it and face the people. By removing the three marble steps leading up to the altar's former position, it was lowered by more than two feet to its present position, closer to the community assembled. On the risers of these steps and those remaining down to the nave, the Latin texts of the Beatitudes had been painted in gold leaf. This painting was removed as part of the altar changes. Also, the beautiful floor mosaics of French stone that had previously been on the top step were carefully removed and restored on the floor behind the altar's new position. These contain symbolic images including a lily and a pelican, an early symbol for Christ.[180] A sedilia was constructed behind the altar for the seating of clergy. This profound change in the placement and function of the altar, hardly noticed by most contemporary visitors to the Chapel, was a local reflection of a worldwide liturgical reform movement of the twentieth century, and it was also part of a wider cultural aspiration of the 1960's and 70's to make institutions more relevant and responsive to the perceived needs of modern life.

The Liturgical reform movement had its roots in the early 1900's as archeological and linguistic experts conducted new and improved research on the early Church, and inevitably scholars and Church leaders sought to

The Very Reverend Ward B. Ewing celebrates Easter Eucharist
with faculty and students.

incorporate these new understandings into liturgical life, setting aside outmoded
and Medieval practices. Adherents to the Liturgical movement sought not to
become Patristic-period fundamentalists, but rather to freshly embrace a number
of newly understood influences, including the early church models and a liturgical
rediscovery of the Bible and the Eucharist.[181] Further, modern times heightened a
sense of the need for community in an industrialized age, as well as a new respect
for the laity and a sense of the power of vernacular expression. The Associated
Parishes movement nurtured a discernment process on liturgical options.[182] The
work of Massey Shepherd and others focused on the essential initiatory nature of
Baptism and the centrality of the Eucharist.[183] As Ruth Meyers has written:

> In these years, 'a liturgical movement' swept through not only the
> Episcopal Church but also other churches of the Anglican Communion,
> the Roman Catholic Church and several mainline Protestant
> churches. It was a time of enormous liturgical ferment, with extensive
> experimentation in virtually every aspect of the liturgy, including
> ritual action, congregational participation, hymnody, architecture, and
> the visual arts.[184]

As this gradually took hold in the Episcopal Church, substantial change began to occur and the stage was set for substantial revisions in the Book of Common Prayer in 1979.[185]

At the Seminary, Dean Rose, Wylie's immediate predecessor, had worried that the strong traditional design and worship practice of the Seminary and the neglected care of the conditions of the Chapel, "retard, rather than advance the spiritual life of the students."[186] After much debate and experimentation, the Board of Trustees with Wylie's encouragement decided that "the sanctuary is to be reconstructed to make possible contemporary as well as traditional forms of worship."[187] For some time celebrants had been permitted to use a temporary free-standing table as an altar facing the community. Deans Rose and Wylie also experimented with the style and schedule of the Chapel's services to allow both "the low churchmen *and* those who accepted the new 'Catholic' customs to acquire a disciplined spiritual life without conforming to a pattern that seems foreign to them."[188] Also a thorough cleaning and a new lighting scheme were ordered, the latter being a gift from St. Thomas Parish on Fifth Avenue. The original electric light sconces from 1897 were removed and contemporary spot lighting was installed to eliminate the "gloom" that Dean Rose had lamented.[189] The well-regarded architects prepared several options for altar renovations before settling on the redesign that remains in place today.[190]

Towering above the altar is the remarkable Gothic reredos, also of alabaster from the famous Royal Quarry at Nottingham, source for many English royal and church projects.[191] Initially the niches in the reredos were left empty, but soon Rhind created the ensemble of figures carved in Italian marble that we know today: the four Gospellers, plus Peter, Paul, Moses and John the Baptist, who flank the central figure of Jesus the Good Shepherd with his two lambs.[192] Each of the Gospellers' symbolic identities—Matthew's angel, Mark's winged lion, Luke's bull and John's eagle—are intriguingly hidden behind their draped figures and peer out at the surprised viewer. Each figure also holds a symbol of his ministry. Peter has the keys to the Church and Luke his gospel manuscript. The reredos is rendered in a lively Gothic style, with lobed niches, corner crockets, traceries of leaves and grapes and pointed arches. The setting is vibrant with energy and movement, "alive with foliage," but the statues themselves have a calm typical of the later

A Hoffman tradition continued, the carving of the names of distinguished faculty in the niches of the sanctuary.

Renaissance.[193] The tool marks visible on the figures make them appear relaxed and add to a sense of quiet graciousness. Each figure was originally crowned with a painted marble nimbus, perhaps the better to connect them to Jesus, who wears one. When one of these fell and cracked, the others were removed; only one remains in the Seminary Archives.[194] The statue of Jesus exhibits a calm and comforting countenance, pleasing and inviting. Thomas notes that "Rhind's skill as a portraitist was utilized by Dean Hoffman in so many ways," including, she suggests, in the double-portrait of Haight the architect as St. Paul.[195] (The photographic evidence of similarity between Haight and the statue of Paul—and the fact that Paul is holding a symbol of his ministry, a small Gothic church—support her claim.)

As planned by Dean Hoffman, within the sanctuary niches on either side of the altar are carved the names and dates of service of prior deans, faculty members and chaplains,

last updated in 1997 after research by the Seminary's senior historian, J. Robert Wright. These are highlighted in gold leaf and reflect Hoffman's understanding of their central importance to the Seminary's mission, and the affection, remembrance and respect which he deemed they deserve.

## *The Word*

AT ITS CONSECRATION AND FOR MORE THAN A DECADE TO FOLLOW, preachers in the Chapel spoke from a small lectern placed on the upper tier of the faculty stalls on the Dean's side of the Chapel (to the right as one faces the altar). In 1906 a genuine pulpit and sound board canopy were designed by Haight and created by Ellis and Kitson. (The small lectern in the stalls continued to be used for many decades for the reading of Scripture at the Offices.) From this historic pulpit, exquisitely carved of New York oak, thousands of sermons have been

Archbishop Desmond Tutu graces the Chapel's pulpit, September 2005.

delivered by a wide range of preachers, including students, faculty, lay leaders, bishops and clergy from across the globe. The preaching practice and the scale and frequency of sermons has varied greatly over the decades. In the nineteenth century extremely long and theologically dense preaching was the norm and then, at later times, very brief homilies, delivered from the broad step of the sanctuary or even the center aisle, were common. In the most recent times, full length, substantive preaching has been the practice, with senior students being invited by the Dean each to take their turn preaching to the entire community. Traditionally, these have been memorable occasions when the students gather and support each other on their day in the Chapel's pulpit. Each faculty member is currently invited to do so each year, as well.

To emphasize the importance of preaching, two annual prizes (along with other treasured academic awards) have long been awarded to students by the faculty. The Seymour Prize (formerly a gold watch) is for the best extemporaneous preaching, and The Bishop of Newark Preaching Prize goes to the competing

Senior with the best sermon. This prize is a small monetary award and includes the honor of preaching at the Baccalaureate Evensong. In recent years, under the leadership of the longstanding Trinity Church Professor of Preaching, Mitties DeChamplain, the Seminary's homiletics program has been quite effective, and students have been artfully guided in finding and developing their individual preaching styles, a confidence they have taken away to parishes all across the country. In the midst of its fine wood, glass and stone the Chapel has been the setting for the consistent preaching of the Word since its Consecration in 1888.


## Aids to Worship


IN ADDITION TO THE MULTIPLE IMAGES in stone, glass, bronze and wood, there are several beautiful traditional Christian images in the Chapel's collection of icons. Long held in great esteem and especially venerated in the Eastern and Russian Churches, icons have a complex history in the West. This is true in part because the artistic expression in icons has a different intention and meaning than other religious paintings or sculpture. As one scholar puts it, "From its very nature, the art of the icon is *liturgical art*: the mystery enacted [in the Eucharist] and the mystery depicted [in the icon] are one. The central truths of faith, celebrated in the liturgy, are also visually set forth in the icons: the Trinity, the Incarnation, the death and Resurrection."[196] Far from being mere ornamental extras, the icons are an essential part of Orthodox practice, "one of the instruments of the knowledge of God, one of the means of communion with him."[197]

This view was not widely held in the West, as the Seminary's Professor of Ecclesiastical History, J. Robert Wright has taught his students of Church history. An expert student and teacher of icons, he notes that although the word *icon* in Biblical Greek "has a rather innocent and broad meaning of simply *image*," the ecclesiastical controversy over the place of religious images in Christian devotion that was fought in the eighth century was an intense and even violent struggle. This so-called Iconoclastic Controversy left its mark on the Church of England. Although pictorial symbolic images of Christian ideas, persons and history had had a long and very early history, many Anglican theologians rejected icons. Their reasons were rooted in scripture and in the liturgical nature and claims of iconic art discussed above, and because they did not make a key theological distinction between the worship of an object and the lesser veneration or the respectful viewing of a holy object. Over time, however, this controversy has faded and in

The icon of Alexander Crummell, a powerful reminder
of racism in the Church.

the late twentieth century, as Wright notes, "Both private and public use of icons among Anglicans has increased considerably in the last decades."[198]

The Chapel now has five icons of holy persons which are displayed and used as aids to worship by some and considered as beautiful curiosities by others. A triptych icon of the Transfiguration has been prominently displayed for many years and rests on the ambo in the center aisle.[199] A stunning icon of the Old Testament Trinity was given to the Chapel by the Orthodox Patriarch of Moscow in thanks for an honorary doctorate degree conferred on him in 1991.[200] A simple icon of Mary the mother of Jesus hangs in the Tower Room. In the Sacristy is a lovely icon of Florence Li Tim-Oi from Hong Kong, who in 1944 was the first woman ordained a priest in the Anglican Communion. This icon was a gift of the class of 2005.[201] And in 1998 the graduating class of the Seminary commissioned an icon of Alexander Crummell, the intellectual African-American who was denied admittance to the Seminary in 1844 because of his race, but eventually became an ordained priest nonetheless and had a distinguished career in the Church that spanned fifty years and three continents. His icon hangs on the sanctuary wall and a candle is lit near it each day. At the Dean's request, Wright prepared and the community celebrated a service for the blessing and dedication of this icon during Evensong on May 15, 1998. Both Li Tim-Oi and Crummell have been honored by placement on the calendar of saints of the Episcopal Church where their full biographies are recorded.[202]

## *Above it All, a Tower Full of Life*

HAIGHT COMPLETED HIS DESIGN FOR THE CHAPEL with a dramatic bell tower, rising 131 feet over Chelsea.[203] Invoking ancient Anglican tradition, the square campanile was closely modeled on the famous tower of Magdalen College, the tallest building in Oxford and a central feature of collegiate life there since around 1500.[204] On each side of Haight's tower, at the belfry, stand pairs of foliated arches separated by stone mullions. Louvers infill the arches and open into a loft where fifteen tubular bells hang. A crenellated parapet tops the tower, with four corner turrets above the parapet, each capped with a pointed finial.

It seems the ten large bells of Magdalen Tower had a particular appeal to Dean Hoffman. He had heard them during several stays in Oxford, and on the day in 1896 when he received his honorary doctoral degree there, the Oxford Society of Change Ringers played a special set of English change-ringing.[205] Hoffman had donated a new peal of bells when he served St. Mark's Parish in Philadelphia.[206] As he planned the Seminary's own Chapel tower, Hoffman was intrigued by the possibility of using tubular bells, a new, lighter, less expensive style of church bells then gaining popularity in England. Tubular bells are long tubes of brass (or other bell metals) and are played with strikers attached to long ropes or cables rung by a chimer far below. In the mid-nineteenth century, an English manufacturer, John Harrington of Coventry, was the sole maker of the new tubular bell chimes for towers. He earned his first patent in 1884, and his bells received much favorable comment in Anglican music circles. Dean Hoffman heard of these developments and asked William Bispham, father of a student, to visit Harrington's factory while in England in order to investigate the new system. A favorable report followed, and Bispham and Hoffman shortly thereafter

traveled to Providence, Rhode Island to meet with Harrington's American agent, Walter Durfee, and to hear the bells for themselves. It was typical that such a choice required Hoffman's personal attention and approval.[207] A commission followed quickly, funded by the Hoffman family, this time in memory of the Dean's parents. The Seminary's tubular bells were among the very first installed in America. Durfee and his competitors eventually placed dozens of such bell systems in colleges and churches in the United States and Canada, including nearby Christ Church in Rye, New York and Vassar College in Poughkeepsie.

Played from the Chimers' loft half-way up the tower, the chimes have been rung daily since their first peals on the day of the Chapel's Consecration in 1888. *The New York Times* reported the next day on the "exceedingly sweet clear chime of bells."[208] The student Guild of Chimers, like the Sacristans and the Precentors, has been a central feature of Seminary life for several generations. The Chimers' unique contribution can be heard at Evensong each day as well as before community Eucharist celebrations. They also play concerts of chimed hymns on specially designated dates of significance to the Hoffman family—or in the life of the Seminary. These include so-called "Hoffman Days," four dates each year on which their key family births, deaths or anniversaries are commemorated. For nearly one hundred years the chimers performed on a particularly challenging pulled-rope system. A more manageable Eijsbouts baton clavier replaced that system in 1983, permitting the striking of the bells through a keyboard-like panel.[209] In 2006 the Chief Chimer and a team of eight guild members laboriously transcribed many hymns for greater ease of playing by novice Chimers.[210] Chimers have traditionally included their own selections of music, and on occasion have even broken into popular music to celebrate the end of examinations or holiday seasons. Their music is one of many features of the Seminary that flows out to the city far beyond Chelsea Square. And it represents a distinctive connection to the Seminary's Anglican roots. Bell towers were historically a regular feature of English parish and scholastic life. The Venerable Bede, the "first historian" of the English Church, reports on the bell tower of St. Hilda's priory in North Yorkshire in the eighth century.[211]

## *Behind the Scenes*

WITH OVER TWENTY SERVICES scheduled in the chapel each week, the necessary preparation, vesting, and gathering constitute important features of Chapel life. The Sacristy has stood at the epicenter of this activity for one hundred and twenty years. A fine if well-worn room, the Sacristy is lined with twenty oak lockers for the vestments of each faculty member and the Chief Sacristan, and a fireplace with a carved marble mantle bearing the Hoffman family crest and motto, *Carpe Diem*. (This crest appears also on the interior and exterior dedication panels over the Chapel's main door and on the exterior of Hoffman Hall.) A particularly striking small stained glass window nearby depicts Jacob wrestling with his angel, and a separate leaded glass window contains the Psalmist's prayer to "Let Thy Priests be Clothed with Righteousness."[212] The celebrants' vestments and the acolytes' cassock-albs (formerly surplices) occupy their own cabinets, as does the collection of vessels and sterling service pieces needed for worship. Sacristans' black cassocks hang on hooks designated by day of the week. A bulletin board holds the various Rota sheets with the schedules designating who is responsible for which of myriad duties. The hymns and canticles for the day are noted, as are the celebrants, deacons and

priests assigned. On the walls of the sacristy two other noteworthy treasures hang: the framed "Instrument of Donation" and the consecration document signed in 1888 by the Seminary secretary and the Presiding Bishop, proclaiming that the chapel should henceforth be under the "spiritual direction of the House of Bishops, and their successors in office."

The ground floor of the tower is known as the Tower Room, where sacristans, faculty, clergy, acolytes, crucifers, thurifers and preachers gather to pause and pray prior to entering the Chapel at the sound of a single bell. Before daily Offices, the Sacristans here lead the praying of the *Angelus* near an icon of Mary with the appropriate chiming, calling the community to the Offices. Since 1888, this room has been a gathering place of seminarians, deans, faculty members, distinguished visitors and preachers. It has known the laughter, prayer and nervous energy that preceded countless moments of worship for generations. A particularly distinctive tradition begins here each weekday as the vested faculty gather for a procession to evening prayer.

On the brick walls of the room have been placed nine tablets commemorating various historic entities: individuals, faculty or donations.[213] The largest is a memorial noting that the "Chime of Fifteen Bells" was given in honor of Glorvina Rossell Hoffmann and Samuel Verplanck Hoffman by their children (including the Dean and his three siblings) and nine grandchildren. Other tablets, taken from

New York's Church of the Annunciation after it was deconsecrated in 1895, honor the memory of Arthur Carey and Samuel Seabury, Jr. The most recent memorials commemorate the gift of new chapel lighting given by St. Thomas Church in 1974; various improvements made in 1984 in honor of Bishop of Pittsburgh Robert B. Appleyard, a Chairman of the Board of Trustees; and the 1992 donation of finely etched glass windows depicting St. Mary and her cousin St. Elizabeth, in the Chapel vestibule, given by Bishop Harold Robinson of Western New York.[214]

# Inspired Endurance

AFTER ONE HUNDRED AND TWENTY YEARS, it is clear that Hoffman's grand aspirations for the Chapel of the Good Shepherd have been realized. His sanctuary stands as an enduring expression of the Anglican faith alive at the seminary today, a faith lived throughout the generations. And Hoffman's Chapel does still more. It proclaims the endurance of a *general* seminary in this city on the Hudson. It makes its proclamation in the best Anglican tradition of confronting differences and struggles with the tools of commitment and energy and prayer. It stands for the continuing vitality of the larger Church, free from partisan and geographic battles, "built to last, built to stay." As Hoffman's predecessor Dean Seymour stated, "The Seminary in the city, never surrender it! It is a grand point. Keep it and struggle for it." [215]

The present dean, Ward B. Ewing, seems to have taken Seymour's admonition fully to heart, as he and the trustees struggle to realize a twenty-first century vision for the Seminary that will keep it at the busy urban intersection of the church, the academy and the society.

In 2005 Dean Ewing and the Archbishop Desmond Tutu stood outside the doors of the Chapel to introduce the most sweeping renovation plans since Hoffman's tenure. They explained that a national conference center, named after the Archbishop, would fill much of the historic group of buildings on the Tenth Avenue boundary of the Seminary. (It is expected to open on September 11, 2007.) It will provide, actually and figuratively, a new and revitalized connection to the city and the world, with meeting spaces and classrooms for vital projects centered around issues of peace and reconciliation, Jewish-Christian dialogue, continuing education and spiritual growth. As Tutu spoke that day, he recalled his residency at General in October 1984 when the Ambassador of Norway arrived to announce that he had been awarded the Nobel Peace Prize. "The Chapel bells were pealing for all they were worth," he said with a twinkling smile. "It was so utterly apt," he said, that after a bustling press conference on the Seminary lawns with the media, "representatives of the world, the secular, the profane, we moved, as one into the Chapel to thank God, a God who embraces all the dichotomies of heaven and the earth, the secular and the sacred." [216]

It is in those dichotomies that the Anglican faith lives, sometimes in great tension, and it is in those separate yet intertwined realities that the Chapel serves

God. Our Chapel may endure as a beloved landmark in the midst of Chelsea, but it has always had a higher purpose as well. At the building's dedication in 1888, the Presiding Bishop of the Episcopal Church, John Williams of Connecticut, performed the consecration and "separated this Chapel henceforth from all unhallowed, worldly and common uses." Separated but never far away, the Chapel of the Good Shepherd still invites all to enter through the gates into the city. [217]

# ENDNOTES

1. When the West Building was built, a gate to the cobbled Twentieth Street was aligned with the now rarely used west door of the building. With the erection of a new permanent retaining wall and fine iron fence, the west gate was moved to align with the Chapel entrance. This Chapel Gate is now one of four that communicate with the city on all four sides of the Seminary.

2. Interview with White, April 2007.

3. Bernice Thomas, *Dean Hoffman's Grand Design,* The General Theological Seminary, New York, 1988, 9. This thorough and carefully researched exhibition documents not only the buildings, but the ministry and art collections of Dean Hoffman.

4. New York City Landmarks Preservation Commission, *Chelsea Historic District Designation Report,* 1981.

5. *Proceedings of The General Convention of The Protestant Episcopal Church,* 1817, 211.

6. The Reverend Creighton Spencer-Mounsey, *Address at the Exercises in Seabury Hall,* The General Theological Seminary, 1935.

7. Moore's authorship of this famous poem has been challenged by the descendants of another 19th century author, Henry Livingston. Their case has been taken up by the literary sleuth, Donald Foster of Vassar College. See: Donald Foster, *Authors Unknown,* Henry Holt, New York, 2000.

8. Higgins and Quasebarth, Architects, New York Historic Preservation Certification Application, New York, September 2005.

9. Edwin G. Burrows and Mike Wallace, *Gotham: A History of New York City to 1898,* Oxford University Press, New York, 1999, 578.

10. In 1892, The East Building was razed to make way for the faculty residences known as Chelsea Square 2/3/4. See: Powel Mills Dawley, *The Story of the General Theological Seminary: A Sesquicentennial History 1817–1967,* Wipf & Stock, Eugene, Oregon, 1969, 260.

11. Marvin Trachtenberg and Isabelle Hyman, *Architecture,* Abrams Publishing, the Netherlands, 1986, 399.

12. Ibid., 401.

13. Émile Mâle, *The Gothic Image,* Icon Editions, 1972.

14. Hugh T. Kerr, "The Gothic Image: Church and College," *Theology Today,* July 1991, 125.

15. Montgomery Schuyler, "The Works of Charles Coolidge Haight," *The Architecture Record,* 1899, The Great American Architects Series, No. 6, 1–83.

16. Ibid.

17. See untitled engraving in the Seminary Archives and *Chelsea Historic District Designation Report,* New York City Landmarks Preservation Commission, 1981. See also survey in Archives of the estates of Clement Clarke Moore and other Chelsea landowners by John Bute Holmes, City Surveyor, 1869.

Note the high and low watermarks of the Hudson River which cut across Chelsea Square. This survey is currently displayed in the Dean's office vestibule.

18. Mark Kurlansky, *The Big Oyster: History of the Half Shell,* Ballantine Books, New York, 2006, xvi.

19. Burrows and Wallace, 447.

20. Ibid., 447.

21. The General Theological Seminary, *Proceedings of Board of Trustees,* Volume V, 341.

22. Dawley, 222.

23. Within the Episcopal Church there was disagreement over these issues, with some taking extreme positions. Many wanted to counter the simplicity of the prevailing style of liturgy, service and settings with more color and embellishment through, for example, the use of more ornamental vestments. See: Sydney E. Ahlstrom, *A Religious History of the American People,* Yale University Press, New Haven, 1972, 621 ff. See also: Nigel Gates, *The Oxford Movement and Anglican Ritualism,* Historical Association, London, 1983.

24. The Rev. John Murray Forbes, The General Theological Seminary, *Report to the Board of Trustees,* May 1871. Proceedings of the Board of Trustees, Vol IV, 441.

25. Dawley, 180.

26. The General Theological Seminary, *Report of the Committee on the Removing of the Seminary,* Proceedings of the Board of Trustees, January 19, 1870, Vol IV, 494.

27. Proceedings of The General Convention of the Protestant Episcopal Church, 1821.

28. The General Theological Seminary, *Report to the Standing Committee of the Seminary,* Proceedings of the Board of Trustees, Vol IV, 487.

29. Ibid., 521.

30. John Murray Forbes, The General Theological Seminary, *The Report on the Removing of the Seminary.*

31. John Murray Forbes, The General Theological Seminary, *Report of the Dean to the Board of Trustees, Proceedings of the Board of Trustees,* Vol IV.

32. The General Theological Seminary, *Report of the Faculty Committee on Discipline and Instruction,* Board of Trustees Proceedings, Vol IV, 627.

33. Ibid., 628.

34. Robert Bruce Mullin, *Episcopal Vision/American Reality: High Church Theology and Social Thought in Evangelical America,* Yale University Press, New Haven, 1986. 162.

35. See an excellent unpublished paper on this topic: Nathanael LeRud, M. Div. 2007, *The Examinations of Arthur Carey,* The General Theological Seminary, 2006, St. Mark's Library.

36. See tone of Forbes' report fn 24. See: Seymour *Defence,* fn 38.

37. James Elliot Lindsley, *This Planted Vine: A Narrative History of the Episcopal Diocese of New York,* Harper & Row, New York, 1984, 235.

38. George F. Seymour, *A Defence of the Professor of Ecclesiastical History Against the Assault of the Dean of the General Theological Seminary,* 1871. A sole copy of this pamphlet is in the Archives. It details, through affidavit-like appendices, "occurrences (sic) which took place in the spring and summer of 1870," which point to Forbes' excesses. In Seymour's apparently passionate handwriting are his assertions of his pain and the truthfulness of his claims.

39. Dawley, 235.

40. Iver Bernstein, *The New York City Draft Riots: Their Significance for American Society and Politics in the Age of the Civil War,* Oxford University Press, New York, 1990, 229.

41. Robert A. M. Stern, Thomas Mellins, David Fishman, *New York 1880, Architecture and Urbanism in the Gilded Age,* Monacelli Press, New York, 1999, "Unprecedented Boom," 48. Burroughs and Wallace, 930.

42. Tom Lewis, *The Hudson: a History,* Yale University Press, New Haven, 2005, 241. Also, Burrows and Wallace, 970.

43. Burrows and Wallace, 945.

44. Stern, et al., for description of the "cast iron aesthetic," 26. Burroughs and Wallace, 946.

45. Stern, et al., 48. for full description of the newly rich. Burroughs and Wallace, 951.

46. Ibid. 663 ff, "Amusements." Burroughs and Wallace, 959.

47. Ken Burns, Episode Three, "Sunshine and Shadow," *New York: A Documentary Film,* Steeplechase Films and WGBH, Boston, 1999.

48. Burroughs and Wallace.

49. Morgan Dix, unpublished diary, entry June 27, 1872, Archives of Trinity Church, New York.

50. The General Theological Seminary, *Proceedings of the Board of Trustees,* Vol IV, 534.

51. The General Theological Seminary, *Triennial Report of the Board of Trustees,* Vol IV, 495.

52. Ibid. Pierrepont was known as the "first citizen" of Brooklyn; one of the first city planners, he was precisely the sort of well-connected Episcopalian to whom the post-Forbes era Board listened.

53. Ibid.

54. Lewis, "River of Fortunes," a complete history of the dramatic building of the Hudson shoreline of Manhattan, 247. Also, Stern, et al. 51.

55. The General Theological Seminary, *Triennial Report of the Board of Trustees,* Vol IV, 537.

56. Ibid.

57. Robert Prichard, *A History of the Episcopal Church,* Morehouse Publishing, Harrisburg, 1999, 144.

58. Ibid.

59. Dawley, 239.

60. The General Theological Seminary, *Dean's Report,* Proceedings of the Board of Trustees Vol IV, 730.

61. Dawley, 247.

62. The General Theological Seminary, *Dean's Report,* Vol IV, 161.

63. Burroughs and Wallace, 1022.

64. Ibid., 1002.

65. The General Theological Seminary, Proceedings of the Board of Trustees, Vol IV, 667.

66. Burroughs and Wallace, 1023.

67. Ibid., 1028.

68. Edwin Palmer Hoyt, *The House of Morgan,* Dodd, Mead, New York, 1966.

69. David McCullough, interviewed in Burns.

70. Ibid.

71. The General Theological Seminary, *Dean's Report,* Proceedings of the Board of Trustees Vol IV, 730.

72. Ibid.

73. The $8,000 annual deficits of this period would measure, in 2007 values, over $150,000 each. www.measuringworth.com

74. Theodore M. Riley, *A Memorial Biography of the Very Reverend Eugene Augustus Hoffman,* Marion Press, New York, 1904.

75. Ibid., 3, 5.

76. Burrows and Wallace, 1036.

77. *Oxford Dictionary of Art,* Ian Childers, ed., Oxford, 2004.

78. Burrows and Wallace, 1086.

79. Walt Whitman, *Complete Poetry and Collected Prose,* Viking Press, New York, 1982. The idea to quote this poem here came from a dramatic reading with powerful New York images found in Ken Burns, *New York: A Documentary Film.*

80. David McCullough in Burns, Episode Three, "Shadow and Light."

81. Ibid.

82. John Steele Gordon, *An Empire of Wealth: The Epic History of American Economic Power,* Harper Collins, New York, 2004. See interview in Burns, "Episode Three, Shadow and Light."

83. McCullough in Burns. Also, Sterns et al., 13 ff.

84. Burrows and Wallace, 1087.

85. Riley, 617.

86. The National Register of Historic Places, The Jekyll Island Historic District, http://www.cr.nps.gov/nr

87. Riley, 775.

88. Lindsley, 229.

89. Riley, 589.

90. The General Theological Seminary, Proceedings of the Board of Trustees, *Annual Report of the Standing Committee,* 1880, Vol V, 297.

91. Unpublished Hoffman correspondence, Archives of the New York Historical Society.

92. The General Theological Seminary, *Report of the Dean,* May 1883. Proceedings of the Board of Trustees, Vol V, 578.

93. Riley, 602.

94. The General Theological Seminary, *Report of the Dean, 1880.* Proceedings of the Board of Trustees, Vol V, 309.

95. Ibid.

96. Ibid.

97. Riley, 622-626.

98. Elizabeth Delude, et al, unpublished study, "St. Ignatius Episcopal Church," Columbia University Graduate School of Architecture and Planning, Spring 1994.

99. *The Haight Family Papers,* The New York Historical Society.

100. Benjamin Haight was elected Bishop of Massachusetts, but withdrew prior to consecration due to ill health. *The Churchman,* October 1873.

101. Thomas, 5.

102. Riley, 627.

103. Montgomery Schuyler, "The Works of Charles Coolidge Haight," *The Architectural Record 1899,* Series 6, 1-83.

104. Alfred Morton Githens, "Charles Coolidge Haight," *Architectural Record,* April 1917, 3074.

105. *The Churchman,* March 13, 1886.

106. Phoebe B. Stanton, *The Gothic Revival and American Church Architecture,* The Johns Hopkins University Press, Baltimore, 1968.

107. Thomas, 6.

108. Ibid.

109. Delude, et al.

110. V. H. H. Green, *A History of Oxford University,* Batsford, Ltd. London, 1974. Plate 1, "Magdalen College Tower," engraving by Michael Burgess (d.1727). Plate 17, "Gate and Chapel Magdalen College," F. Mackenzie, 1826. Also, Cyril M. Harris ed., *Illustrated Historic Architecture,* Dover, New York, 1977. Also, Howard Colvin, *Unbuilt Oxford,* Yale University Press, New Haven, 1983, 98 ff.

111. Riley, 622.

112. Dawley, 225.

113. Ibid.

114. Higgins and Quasebarth.

115. Schuyler, 75.

116. *The Churchman,* April 17, 1880.

117. Dawley, 260.

118. Thomas, 14.

119. Ibid., 5.

120. Eugene. A. Hoffman, "An Appeal," *The Churchman,* April 17, 1880.

121. Riley, 597.

122. Ibid., 611.

123. For fuller excerpt of *The New York Times* editorial see Riley, 614.

124. Thomas, 16.

125. Thomas, 9.

126. *The New York Times,* November 1, 1888.

127. Alfred Morton Githens, ed., *The Group Plan,* "The Brick Builder," New York, 1900.

128. Interview with White, April 2006.

129. "Blessed are they that do his commandments, that they may have right to the tree of life, and may enter in through the gates into the city." Revelations 22:14. King James Version.

130. Raymond E. Brown, *An Introduction to The New Testament,* Doubleday, New York, 1997, 794.

131. Stuart Kenworthy, "The Chapel of the Good Shepherd: A Sacred Space of Intimacy or Distance?" "It is interesting to note the lack of attention that [the meaning and content] of the doors receive." Unpublished 1982 M. Div. thesis, St. Marks Library.

132. Dawley, fn 15, 259. Tympanum by Gorham.

133. Hugh Braun, *An Introduction to English Medieval Architecture,* Faber and Faber, London, 1951, 133.

134. See: The Smithsonian Archives of American Art, www.siris.si.edu, supra note 136.

135. Thomas, 16.

136. Philip Ward-Jackson, *Public Sculpture of the City of London,* Liverpool University Press, 2003. See also *American Art Journal Who's Who 1933,* New York.

137. Thayer Tolles, "American Bronze Casting," *Timeline of Art History,* Metropolitan Museum of Art, New York, 2000.

138. Felix Markham, *Oxford,* Weidenfeld and Nicholson, London, 1967, Plate 8, 141. Also, photographs at www.keble.ox.ac.uk

139. The General Theological Seminary, Archives.

140. George W. Kirk, *The Church Eclectic,* 1888.

141. Braun, 141.

142. The Sacristans' annual "Great Cleaning" on Holy Saturday provides an opportunity to inspect the angels, eye to eye.

143. From another passage of *Revelations*, "'I am the Alpha and the Omega,' says the Lord God, who is and who was and who is to come, the Almighty." Rev. 1:8 (NRSV) The Chi Rho is one of the earliest cruciform symbols. It is formed by superimposing the first two letters of the word Christ in Greek. Although not technically a cross, the Chi Rho invokes the crucifixion. The Greek Cross, with four equal arms, is used to signify the united Church rather than Christ and his sacrifice. Ferguson, supra note 180.

144. Nine virtues are inscribed on the Chapel floor: the four "Cardinal Virtues" from the Platonic traditions, *Justice, Fortitude, Temperance and Prudence;* plus two "Holy Virtues," *Humility and Mercy,* and the three "Theological Virtues" from I Corinthians, *Faith, Hope and Love/Charity.* A quatrefoil is a design with four lobes, sometimes appearing as flower or leaves. *A Dictionary of Architecture and Landscape Architecture,* James Stevens Curl, ed., Oxford University Press, New York, 2006.

145. Alice Elwood, *Dean Hoffman's "Grand Design": Docent Manual* General Theological Seminary,1988.

146. Riley, 700.

147. Dawley, 264.

148. Eugene A. Hoffman, *Digest of the Rules and Regulations of The General Theological Seminary Relating to the Students Compiled for their use by the Dean,* The General Theological Seminary, 1893.

149. *The Illustrated American,* December 6, 1890. Unnamed student quote.

150. Riley, 643.

151. Riley, 687.

152. Eugene A. Hoffman, *The Churchman,* June, 26, 1886.

153. *Illustrated American,* December 6, 1890.

154. S.B. Serle, Vicar of Chislehurst, *The Sacristan and the Server, Plain Guides to Lay Work,* SPCK, London, 1927.

155. *The G.T.S. Sacristan's Manual,* The General Theological Seminary, extant copy dated "Advent, 1934."

156. *The Illustrated American,* December 6,1890.

157. Interview with Professor David Hurd, January 2007.

158. Ibid.

159. David Hurd, Professor of Church Music, sermon November 3, 2004. See: infra note 169. See also, *The New York Times,* November 1, 1888.

160. Nicholas Thistlewaite and Geoffrey Webber, *The Cambridge Companion to the Organ,* Cambridge University Press, 1998, 14.

161. David Hurd, The General Theological Seminary, Music class notes. The taste for "large, louder, more symphonic organs required increased wind pressure" and greater physical strength to play each note. To assist the organist, a mechanism was developed that used the organ's own wind pressure.

162. Dawley, 337.

163. Hurd interview, January 2007.

164. Carl Weinrich, *Bach Organ Music,* Radio Corporation of America, 1962, LM/LSC-2557, Library of Congress catalog, R61-1234, liner notes.

165. Ibid.

166. Peter D'Angio, "The Stained Glass Windows of The Chapel of The Good Shepherd," unpublished thesis for M. Div., April 26, 1994, St. Mark's Library.

167. Ibid., 1.

168. Riley, 512.

169. John Williams, Bishop of Connecticut, Pamphlet prepared regarding the Consecration of The Memorial Chapel of the Good Shepherd, The General Theological Seminary, October 31, 1888.

170. Thomas, 12.

171. For detailed history of this firm, see D'Angio.

172. *The Grove Dictionary of Art,* Oxford University Press, 1996.

173. James Cheshire, *Stained Glass and the Victorian Gothic Revival,* Manchester University Press, 2004, 172.

174. *The Oxford Dictionary of Art,* Ian Childers, ed., Oxford, 2004.

175. For a complete discussion of the direction of worship see: U.M. Lang, *Turning Towards the Lord: Orientation in Liturgical Prayer,* Ignatius Press, San Francisco, 2004, 35.

176. D'Angio, 48.

177. Ibid., 49.

178. Ibid., 52.

179. Ibid., 18.

180. George Ferguson, *Signs and Symbols in Christian Art,* Oxford University Press, 1976, 23, 33. "The lily is the symbol of purity and has become the flower of the Virgin." And the Pelican is known for loving its offspring, even to the point of sharing blood for nourishment. The pelican is sometimes shown in art nesting on the top of a cross. Psalm 102:6 reads "I am like a Pelican of the Wilderness." (KJV)

181. Michael Moriarty, *The Liturgical Revolution, Prayer Book Revision and The Associated Parishes: A Generation of Change in the Episcopal Church,* The Church Hymnal Corp., New York, 1996.

182. Ibid., 44. The Associated Parishes collaboration was founded at the College of Preachers, Washington, D. C., November 1946. "Our job is to stir up divine discontent with the way things are done," said John O. Patterson, rector from Wisconsin.

183. Massey H. Shepherd, Jr., *The Worship of the Church,* Seabury Press, New York, 1952.

184. Ruth Meyers, "The Emergence of a Eucharistic Ecclesiology," *Continuing the Reformation: Re-Visioning Baptism in the Episcopal Church,* Church Publishing, 1997, 20 ff.

185. The revision of the American prayer book began in 1964 and was approved at the General Convention of 1976. This important liturgical effort is well documented. See: Marion Hatchett, *Commentary on the American Prayer Book,* Harper Collins, New York, 1995. *The Prayer Book Renewal: Worship and the new Book of Common Prayer,* H. Barry Evans, ed., Seabury Press, New York, 1978. *The Prayer Book Studies Series,* various dates, The Standing Liturgical Commission of the General Convention. Jeffrey Lee, *Opening the Prayer Book,* Church Teaching Series, Cowley Publishing, Cambridge, 1999.

186. The General Theological Seminary, *Proceedings of the Board of Trustees,* 1966, 25. See also the evocative unpublished paper, J. Gregory Tallant, M. Div. 2007, "A Swinging Night with Evensong," St. Mark's Library.

187. The General Theological Seminary, *Proceedings of the Board of Trustees,* 1967, 28.

188. The General Theological Seminary, *Proceedings of the Board of Trustees,* 1966, 25. See also: "Chapel Service Revised," *GTS Bulletin,* Vol 53, No 3, May 1967, 1.

189. Two of the original 1897 electric light fixtures remain in use under the organ pipe shelf.

190. See Moore and Hutchins design work in Archives.

191. "A reredos is an ornamented altarpiece, a wall-like screen which rises from the ground level behind a Christian altar." *Oxford Dictionary of Art,* Ian Childers, ed. Oxford, 2004.

192. There has been oral debate on whether the John the Baptist figure is not in fact meant to depict the prophet Elijah, the thought being that Moses (the Law) would balance Elijah (the Prophet). A review of dozens of artistic images of John and Elijah indicate that clearly Rhind intended to render the former here.

193. Thomas and interview with Margaret H. Schwartz, Senior Vice President, Sotheby's, New York.

194. See: Archives. One intact nimbus/halo remains.

195. Thomas, 18.

196. Nicholas Gendle, "Windows of Eternity: The Theology of Icons," from Linette Martin, *Sacred Doorways,* Paraclete Press, Brewster, Massachusetts, 2002, 230.

197. V. Lossky and L. Ouspensky, *The Meaning of Icons,* Olten Press, 1952, 33.

198. J. Robert Wright, unpublished notes regarding icons.

199. This icon was written by the Rev. John Walsted of Staten Island and was the gift of the Rev. Leslie J.A. Lang.

200. J. Robert Wright unpublished notes regarding icons. The Old Testament Trinity subject is best known from a famous icon written by the Russian St. Andrew Rublev in the early fifteenth century. This icon is more properly called "The Hospitality of Abraham," a reference to Genesis 18 in which three angels appear to Abraham at Mamre.

201. The writing of the icon of Florence Li Tim-Oi was done by the Rev. Ellen Francis, OSH.

202. *Lesser Feasts and Fasts,* Church Publishing, New York, 2003. The Crummell icon was written by the Rev. John Walsted.

203. Height confirmed by architects Beyer, Binder and Bell in a 2006 measurement.

204. Supra note 110.

205. The Society is made up of students and clergy and was established in 1734 to rings peals on the bells of the several Oxford University towers. See: Riley for details of various Hoffman trips to Oxford.

206. Riley, 526.

207. Riley, 585ff. At present, one may visit www.gts.edu to hear and see the chimes.

208. *The New York Times,* November 1, 1888.

209. Royal Eijsbouts Company is a 100+ year-old Dutch manufacturer of bells, carillons and systems.

210. A Chief of the Guild of Chimers, Stephen Shaver, M. Div. 2007, organized this effort.

211. Bede, *Ecclesiastical History of the English People,* Penguin Books edition, London, 1990.

212. Genesis 32: 24–30 and Psalm 132:9.

213. See supra note 169.

214. Below the Tower Room, a narrow and dark stair leads to the undercroft and storage area, as well as the labyrinthine tunnels connecting the buildings on the Close.

215. The General Theological Seminary, *Seymour Address* at Sherred Hall dedication, May 1883, Archives.

216. The General Theological Seminary, Archbishop Desmond Tutu remarks, on video, Archives.

217. The document of Consecration of the Chapel hangs on the Sacristy wall. It is signed by the Seminary Secretary and the Presiding Bishop.

# WORKS AND
# INTERVIEWS CITED

Ahlstrom, Sydney E., *A Religious History of the American People,* Yale University Press, New Haven, 1972.

Bede, *Ecclesiastical History of the English People,* Penguin Books, London, 1990.

Bernstein, Iver, *The New York Draft Riots: Their Significance for American Society and Politics in the Age of the Civil War,* Oxford University Press, New York, 1990.

Braun, Hugh, *An Introduction to English Medieval Architecture,* Faber and Faber, London, 1951.

Brown, Raymond E., *An Introduction to the New Testament,* Doubleday, New York, 1997.

Burns, Ken, *New York: A Documentary Film,* Steeplechase Films and WGBH, Boston, 1999.

Burrows, Edwin G. and Mike Wallace, *Gotham: A History of New York City to 1898,* Oxford University Press, New York, 1999.

*The Churchman,* periodical, New York, various dates.

Childers, Ian, *The Oxford Dictionary of Art,* Oxford, 2004.

Cheshire, James, *Stained Glass and the Victorian Gothic Revival,* Manchester University Press, 2004.

Colvin, Howard, *Unbuilt Oxford,* Yale University Press, New Haven, 1983.

Curl, James Stevens, ed., *A Dictionary of Architecture and Landscape Architecture,* Oxford University Press, New York, 2006.

D'Angio, Peter, "The Stained Glass Windows of the Chapel of the Good Shepherd," unpublished thesis, 1994. The General Theological Seminary, St. Mark's Library.

Dawley, Powel Mills, *The Story of the General Theological Seminary: A Sesquicentennial History 1817–1967,* Wipf & Stock, Eugene, Oregon, 1969.

Delude, Elizabeth, et al, unpublished study, "St. Ignatius Episcopal Church," Columbia University Graduate School of Architecture and Planning, 1994.

Dix, Morgan, unpublished diary, Archives of Trinity Church, New York.

Elwood, Alice, *Dean Hoffman's "Grand Design": Docent Manual,* The General Theological Seminary, New York, 1988.

The General Convention of the Protestant Episcopal Church, *Proceedings,* 1817.

The General Theological Seminary of the Episcopal Church, New York. Various volumes of *The Proceedings of the Board of Trustees* and various *Reports* to and from the Board and its Committees and Reports to and from various deans and faculty members. Archives.

*The G.T.S. Sacristans Manual,* The General Theological Seminary, New York, circa 1934.

Foster, Donald, *Authors Unknown,* Henry Holt, New York, 2000.

Ferguson, George, *Signs and Symbols in Christian Art,* Oxford University Press, 1976.

Gates, Nigel, *The Oxford Movement and Anglican Ritualism,* Historical Association, London, 1983.

Githens, Alfred Morton, "Charles Coolidge Haight," *Architectural Record,* 1917.

Githens, Alfred Morton, "The Group Plan," *The Brick Builder*, New York, 1900.

Gordon, John Steele, *An Empire of Wealth: The Epic History of American Economic Power*, Harper Collins, New York, 2004.

Green, V.H.H., *A History of Oxford University*, Batsford, Ltd., London, 1974.

*Grove Dictionary of Art*, Oxford University press, 1996.

Harris, Cyril M., ed., *Illustrated Historic Architecture*, Dover, New York, 1977.

Higgins and Quasebarth, Architects, *New York Historic Preservation Certification Application*, New York, 2005.

Hoffman, Eugene Augustus, unpublished correspondence, The New York Historical Society archives.

Hoffman, Eugene Augustus, *Digest of Rules*, The General Theological Seminary, New York, 1893.

Holmes, John Bute, Survey of the properties of Clarke Clement Moore and other Chelsea property owners, New York, 1869. The General Theological Seminary, Archives.

Hoyt, Edwin Palmer, *The House of Morgan*, Dodd, Mead, New York, 1966.

Hurd, David, interviewed by author, January 2007.

Hurd, David, unpublished notes on organs, 2004.

*Illustrated American*, periodical, New York, 1890.

Kenworthy, Stuart, unpublished thesis, "The Chapel of the Good Shepherd: A Sacred Space of Intimacy or Distance?" 1982, St. Marks Library.

Kerr, Hugh T., "The Gothic Image: Church and College," *Theology Today*, July 1991.

Kirk, George W., periodical, *The Church Eclectic*, 1888.

Kurlansky, Mark, *The Big Oyster: History of the Half Shell*, Ballantine Books, New York, 2006.

Lang, U.M., *Turning Toward the Lord: Orientation in Liturgical Prayer*, Ignatius Press, San Francisco, 2004.

LeRud, Nathanael, "The Examinations of Arthur Carey," unpublished paper, 2006, Archives.

Lewis, Tom, *The Hudson: a History*, Yale University Press, New Haven, 2005.

*Lesser Feasts and Fasts*, Church Publishing, New York, 2003.

Lindsley, James Elliott, *This Planted Vine: A Narrative History of the Episcopal Diocese of New York*, Harper and Row, New York, 1984.

Lossky, V. and L. Ouspensky, *The Meaning of Icons*, Olten Press, Switzerland, 1952.

Markham, Felix, *Oxford*, Weidenfeld and Nicholson, London, 1967.

McCullough, David, interviewed by Ken Burns, *New York: A Documentary Film*, Steeplechase Films and WGBH, Boston, 1999.

Martin, Linette, *Sacred Doorways*, Paraclete Press, Brewster, Massachusetts, 2002.

Mâle, Émile, *The Gothic Image*, Icon Editions, Boulder, Colorado, 1972.

Meyers, Ruth, *Continuing the Reformation: Re-Visioning Baptism in the Episcopal Church*, Church Publishing, 1997.

Moriarty, Michael, *The Liturgical Revolution, Prayer Book Revision and The Associated Parishes: A Generation of Change in the Episcopal Church*, The Church Hymnal Corporation, 1996.

Mullin, R. Bruce, *Episcopal Vision / American Reality: High Church Theology and Social Thought in Evangelical America*, Yale University Press, New Haven, 1986.

National Register of Historic Places, www.cr.nps.gov/nr

New York City Landmarks Preservation Commission, *Chelsea Historic District Designation Report*, New York, 1981.

*The New York Times*, New York, various dates.

Prichard, Robert, *A History of the Episcopal Church,* Morehouse Publishing, Harrisburg, Pennsylvania, 1999.

Riley, Theodore M., *A Memorial Biography of the Very Reverend Eugene Augustus Hoffman,* Marion Press, New York, 1904.

Schuyler, Montgomery, "The Works of Charles Coolidge Haight," *The Architecture Record,* The Great American Architect Series, No 6, 1899.

Serle, S.B., *The Sacristan and the Server, Plain Guides to Lay Work,* SPCK, London, 1927.

Seymour, George F., "A Defence of the Professor of Ecclesiastical History Against the Assault of the Dean of The General Theological Seminary," 1871, Archives.

Shepherd, Massey H., *The Worship of the Church,* Seabury Press, New York, 1952.

Smithsonian Archives of American Art, Washington, www.siris.si.edu

Spencer-Mounsey, Creighton, *Address at the Exercises at Seabury Hall,* The General Theological Seminary, New York, 1935.

Stanton, Phoebe B., *The Gothic Revival and American Church Architecture,* The Johns Hopkins University Press, Baltimore, 1968.

Stern, Robert A.M. and Thomas Mellins, David Fishman, *New York 1880: Architecture and Urbanism in the Gilded Age,* Monacelli Press, New York, 1999.

Thistlewaite, Nicholas and Geoffrey Webber, *The Cambridge Companion to the Organ,* Cambridge University Press, 1998.

Thomas, Bernice, *Dean Hoffman's Grand Design,* The General Theological Seminary, New York, 1988.

Tolles, Thayer, "American Bronze Casting," *Timeline of Art History,* Metropolitan Museum of Art, New York, 2000.

Trachtenberg, Marvin and Isabelle Hyman, *Architecture,* Abrams Publishing, The Netherlands, 1986.

Tutu, Desmond, Remarks at the General Theological Seminary, New York, September 2005, on video, Archives.

Ward-Jackson, Philip, *Public Sculpture of London,* Liverpool University Press, 2003.

Weinrich, Carl, *Bach Organ Music,* Radio Corporation of America, 1962.

Whitman, Walt, *Complete Poetry and Collected Prose,* Viking Press, New York, 1982.

White, Samuel, Interview with author at The General Theological Seminary, New York, April 2006.

Williams, John, "Consecration of the Memorial Chapel of the Good Shepherd," The General Theological Seminary, New York, 1888.

Wright, J. Robert, unpublished notes on icons, St. Marks Library.

PHOTOGRAPH AND ILLUSTRATION ACKNOWLEDGEMENTS

The endpapers are details from the architectural drawings of Charles Coolidge Haight in the Collection of The St. Mark's Library. ◆ The photographs on both page 12 and page 65 are by Pach Brothers. ◆ The illustration on page 16 is from *Harper's Magazine,* January 12, 1889. ◆ The photograph on page 19 is by Lawrence Thornton. ◆ The photograph on page 23 was reproduced from a postcard published by The Elite Stationery Company in September 1913. ◆ The portrait of Dean Hoffman by Eastman Johnson reproduced on page 29 dates from 1882 and was a gift to the Seminary from Eugene A. Hoffman and Margaret E. Hoffman, grandchildren of the Dean. ◆ The photograph of Charles Coolidge Haight on page 35 is a photograph from the Haight Family Papers, Manuscripts, negative number 79361. Collection of the New-York Historical Society. ◆ All color photographs were taken by Bruce Parker between the years 1981 and 2007. ◆ All black and white photographs are from the archives of the Seminary's Communications Office, scanned and digitally restored by Chad Rancourt and Bruce Parker. Except for those noted above, other vintage photographs are without attribution.

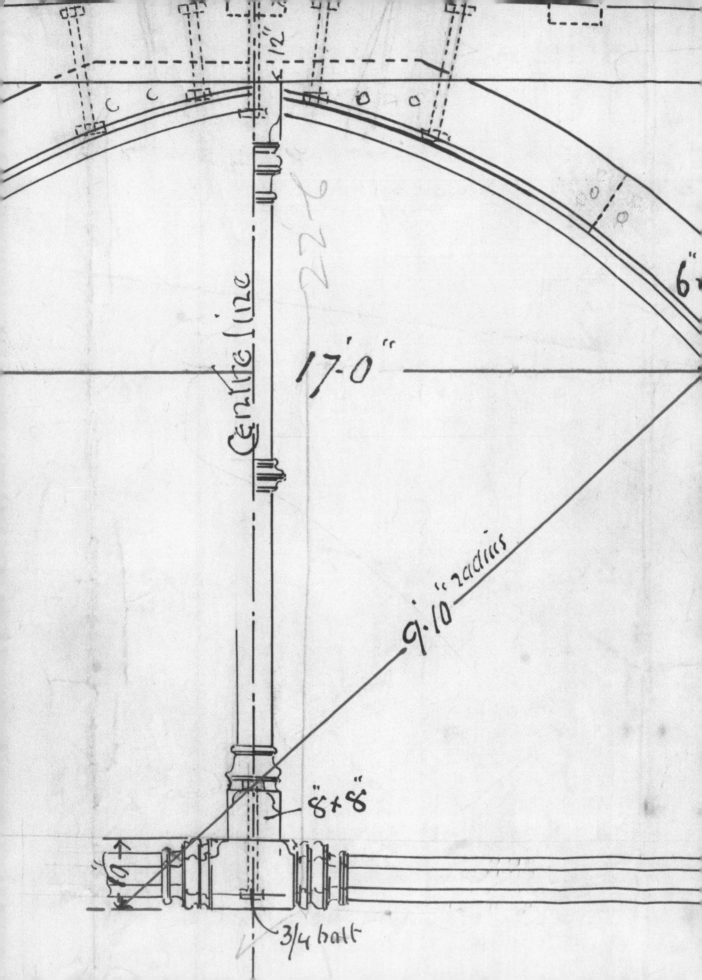

12"

22½

6"

Centre line

17'0"

9.10" radius

8"+8"

10

3/4 bolt